FEAR LESS

Praise for Dr Pippa Grange and *Fear Less*:

'So many of our negative emotions are ultimately driven by fear. In this incredibly personal, powerful book, Pippa Grange shows us how to face our fears and live free, fulfilled lives. A revelation'
Fearne Cotton

'Any of us, including the world's top sports stars, can be held back by fear of failure. Dr Pippa Grange helps us tell different stories about ourselves, so we can be happier, more successful, and more connected to those we love'
Dr Rangan Chatterjee

'We all have and will inevitably encounter some kind of fear in our lives. This book took me to the why, and is rich in techniques on how to overcome it. An outstanding read'
Juan Mata

'Pippa Grange made the England team fearless'
The Times

'A stimulating book for performance and life. We all need to understand fear, and learn how to create the right environment to be courageous. Quality read!'
Eddie Jones

'Practical, powerful, profound. Pippa Grange promises freedom from whatever it is that holds you back'
James Kerr, bestselling author of *Legacy: What the All Blacks Can Teach Us About the Business of Life*

FEAR LESS

HOW TO WIN *YOUR* WAY IN WORK AND LIFE

DR PIPPA GRANGE

Vermilion

This edition published by Vermilion in 2021
First published by Vermilion in 2020

3

Vermilion, an imprint of Ebury Publishing
20 Vauxhall Bridge Road,
London SW1V 2SA

Vermilion is part of the Penguin Random House group of companies
whose addresses can be found at global.penguinrandomhouse.com

www.penguin.co.uk

A CIP catalogue record for this book is available from the British Library

ISBN 9781785042928

Printed and bound in Great Britain by Clays Ltd, Elcograf S.p.A.

The authorised representative in the EEA is Penguin Random House Ireland,
Morrison Chambers, 32 Nassau Street, Dublin D02 YH68.

Penguin Random House is committed to a sustainable future
for our business, our readers and our planet. This book is made
from Forest Stewardship Council® certified paper.

For Ablaye, whose feet-on-the-ground perspective and love of life are truly inspiring. Your example reminds me how much we gain from living a fear less life.

Contents

Contents

Part 4: Replacing *not-good-enough* fear

Foreword

What if I told you that your life is run by fear?

That might chime with you, or it might seem unlikely.

Either way, if you don't feel fulfilled or truly successful, I can promise you that fear is ultimately what's holding you back. If you are quick to judge others or harsh on yourself, fear is speaking. If your life never feels enough, fear is the culprit.

I have spent 20 years working as a performance psychologist, helping people find better, happier ways to work and play. And the conclusion I have reached is that all of us are driven by fear. All of us.

Yet, strangely, that's not a depressing revelation or a permanent life sentence. In fact, once you acknowledge the role of fear, it quickly leads to a truly radical conclusion: if you can shrink the effects of fear, your life will be transformed. That is why working with fear has become the bedrock of what I do.

But first let me explain how I got to this place. My job involves working with leaders and athletes, CEOs and performers, counselling them to get through difficulty or to build resilience and, of course, to succeed and to win. I've spent most of my time in locker rooms and boardrooms, trackside, poolside, pitchside and courtside, often as a sole woman within a team of men.

Ten years ago I noticed my approach changing. I began to see that the real shifts weren't happening at the level of performance – coping, toughing it out, battling to win – but at a deeper level. In my daily conversations, the same themes would come up time and time again: shame, inadequacy, loneliness, jealousy, dissatisfaction. These felt very familiar in my life – I'd imagine they might be in yours, too.

For instance, I would speak to athletes soon after they'd smashed personal bests or even world records. Rather than being full of joy, they would already be feeling pressure around the next race, the next challenge. Or I'd talk to an incredibly successful business leader who'd accumulated all the status symbols of success, but they would only be able to see their own faults.

I also worked with people who had missed out on a trophy or a big opportunity, but who nonetheless weren't broken. In each conversation, I'd try to go deeper, to get to the root of what was happening for these people. I wanted to know why some people felt unfulfilled even as they succeeded, and others felt fulfilled even in failure.

Digging down, what I found underneath was *fear*. I realised that fear appears in our life in many guises. And it's these hidden fears that drive us to feel our lives aren't enough, that prompt us to spend our time worrying about competition, comparison, chasing targets and seeking status, being a perfectionist or over-controlling. Fear turns life into a battle, tells us we need to hide our real selves, that we can never *have* enough or *be* enough.

So, I thought, is there a way to change this? What might living with less fear look like?

I started by looking inwards. I realised that I too had grown up with fear at the heart of my being. I was a council-house kid in a single-parent family that had its issues with alcohol and drug addiction, as well as domestic violence, and I had lost a brother to suicide. Through all of this, my mum, my earliest role model, adopted a Churchillian 'fight them on the beaches' stance, interspersed with bouts of giving up. I grew up thinking being fearless meant shutting down emotionally and toughing it out.

I acted like a smart-arse, mainly to keep people from getting too close. Yet on the inside I was a reserved, studious nerd. And that was my ticket out: I got myself into college, and then, with the help of an inspirational lecturer, to university, all the way to two doctoral degrees – one completed, the other one still ongoing – and some incredible jobs working with top sports teams around the world, from New Zealand rugby league to Australian swimming and football in England, as well as a whole raft of Australian rules football teams.

Although from the outside I looked like a high-achiever, on the inside I did not feel fulfilled – just like the people I was having conversations with. My underlying fear left me believing I had to fight to win at life, to fake it, to hide who I really was.

During these one-on-one conversations with people successful in their field, I kept coming up against fear, in all its different and destructive forms. So I started to look for ways we can talk about fear, to explore underneath the surface issues that were showing up, such as jealousy or dissatisfaction, self-judgement or perfectionism.

I found ways to get to the hidden fear, and to put it in its place. Ways that we can all finally feel fulfilled.

Then, during my work with teams and organisations, I realised fear was both inside us and outside us. I talked to groups about issues that affected everyone's performance, from racism, drugs and alcohol to resilience and mental health. I found that while fear happens in each of our heads, it is also fuelled and recycled by our culture: that is, the beliefs we've adopted, our relationships and environments.

That's why for the last ten years I have positioned myself as a *culture* coach rather than performance psychologist. Individual focus is important too but what makes the biggest difference, in my experience, is culture change.

This book is based on a combination of both my culture and individual work: it's a 360-degree look at how you can see, face and dig up all the sources of fear in your life, inside and out. It includes stories of people that will help you reflect upon your issues, and hopefully leave you feeling optimistic that you *can* do this.

I am profoundly grateful for the deeply personal stories and vulnerability that so many athletes, leaders and coaches I've worked with have shared with me over the years. I'm also grateful to them for the lessons they've taught me and for being brave enough to do this work. Now you can use this set of ideas to stop fear running your life, too.

Let's get started.

Introduction

When was the last time you were *really* scared? You might think: that time I lost my child in a shopping centre; the moment the doctor told me it was serious; the night I was followed home from the bus stop; as I was walking up to the stage to give my big speech.

You are right: all of those are moments that can prompt good old-fashioned fear. What you probably won't instantly recall is all the other times when fear is present inside you. The many moments when fear has been controlling you, without you knowing it.

It's there when you feel unfulfilled, as if there's something missing. When no amount of success, trophies or status symbols is ever quite enough. And it's also there when you feel jealous, judge people, are overcome by perfectionism, or feel the need to crush a colleague.

Fear is way more present in your life than you might think. In fact, it's become our behavioural GPS, mapping out our choices and limiting our possible futures. And it's not all coming from you: so much of how we live and what we believe is coming from outside us, recycled and projected onto us through the cultures we live in.

This book seeks to liberate you from the daily intrusions of fear that are keeping you stuck. And, along with that, to liberate you from fear's accomplices: jealousy, staying separate, perfectionism, shame and being judgemental.

There are two types of fear. There is the jolt-of-adrenalin, panicky, can't-breathe type of fear you can't fail to recognise. This is the kind that happens in a crisis or a moment of high stress, for example a job interview or before a speech or taking a free throw. I call this *in-the-moment* fear, and later in the book I will explain how to calm it.

But most of the book is about the other type of fear, the kind that's running your life, making your choices, leaving you unfulfilled. I call this *not-good-enough* fear.

This is when the emotion of fear gets mixed up with what happened in the past and what might happen in the future. So it's the fear of disappointing people and failing. Of not being good enough. Of not being loved.

Those fears become distorted into the kind of behaviours I named before: jealousy, perfectionism, staying separate and isolated, and staying smaller than we really are. As you read this book, I hope to help you uncover and liberate you from fear as it appears in your life. I want to help you see the fear messages you've created, taken in and live by, and the fear-filled environments you live in.

I have seen what happens when you learn to boss fear instead of it bossing you. I've seen this shift work its magic on the pitch, field and court and also in life, work and relationship situations. I have seen teams turn around from fragmented, individualistic and excuse-making groups to bonded, passionate and unbeatable units. I have seen unfulfilled, struggling or bitter people transform their lives and their performances dramatically.

Facing your fears is a kind of growing up. It's about shedding your parents' fears, your generational and social fears. It will leave you free to explore your true ambitions and rediscover what winning in life means to you. It will help you to look at the world in a new way, with both clarity and optimism.

I have a name for what happens when your need to be successful is driven by a need to beat others, by a fear of not being enough: winning shallow. In this book, I want to reorient you away from this skinny, depriving mentality.

I know that the practice I coach now is sustainable, life-affirming and positive. It's a way of winning that leads you to surprising joy, connection and belonging. I call this kind of success winning deep.

When we win deep, it has all the blood, sweat and tears in it that we think it should, but it's not about individual dominance any more. It is about human passion and ambition, fulfilment and finally feeling that life is enough. It's living a fear-less life.

How to use this book

This is not the usual kind of 'self-help' book. You won't find a cure-all technique to apply to all your problems, or ten tricks to get rid of fear, or any quick fixes.

I don't like those approaches because, in my work as a sports psychologist, I have learned they simply are not a permanent solution for the distorted fear of not being good enough. If you've tried to achieve long-term change by using psychological tricks, you've probably already discovered that for yourself. Techniques have value, but in specific ways, as we will see through Part 1 of the book.

This book is more a collection of ideas and experiences. As you read about other people's experiences, their stories and how they have overcome fear, my hope is that they will help you reimagine how fear plays out in your life, and what you can do or how you can change. Some particular moments, elements or pieces of other people's jigsaw puzzles will chime with you, or feel like possible approaches to a particular situation that will work for you. I believe those deep moments of understanding stay with us far longer than trying to reshape our lives through a trick or a technique.

We tend to put all our focus on logic and evidence. But the deep and lasting work to make fear play a much smaller part in your life will also happen at the level of your unconscious, and it will take effort to get there, and time to bed in. So I'm sorry to say that it probably won't all be sorted by next week.

You might be thinking, 'this sounds like hard work'. Well, hopefully not. The good news is there's no need for you do to exercises or homework: you just have to read, reflect, and let your imagination and unconscious start doing their thing.

The other good news is you won't find reams of data and proof in these pages. I've written from a lived place, from being in the field. That's because I want to turn your attention away from facts and figures for a moment and inwards towards what you know in your soul – again, into the place where the work happens, your unconscious.

The breakthroughs in someone's performance, or a spike in joy, confidence and fulfilment, don't just come from thinking, or from evidence and theories. In a relationship or group, they come from having enough love in the room – a vibe of genuine warmth, close relationship and a desire for the other person to find his or her best. On a personal level, they come from you being willing to have a really good look at what part fear is playing in your life. And they come from the wisdom of your imagination and instinct, and from that wildly unscientific place: soul.

It is scary to talk about soul or love in our hyper-rational, data-driven world, but I am convinced these are the missing pieces in our potential, and in fighting fear. This is the only genuine way to talk about change and becoming fearless.

The other problem with much pop-psychology and self-help is that it focuses primarily on us as isolated individuals, trapped in our thoughts. That's only part of the puzzle. Fear happens inside us, but it also comes from outside: from our environments, school, work, teams, families, relationships.

Ironically, you might think those fear emotions and behaviours I have described – jealousy, perfectionism, staying separate and negative judgements – are only happening in your own head. That they are your own shameful secret. In reality, those behaviours, thoughts and feelings are happening in all of our heads.

There is no meaningful difference between how men and women naturally respond to fear, but there are differences in how we are socialised to respond to it. Society often teaches boys – even when as a parent we don't mean to – to be more 'tough', that they shouldn't express their emotions, including fear. So a woman may be more likely to show when she is scared. But when it comes to distorted fears, men and women are much more similar than different. We all struggle with our own personal manifestations of those fear emotions, rooted in our fear of not being good enough.

In the first part of the book, I'll ask you to look at the fear-provoking cultures and environments we all live in, and to think about how they affect you. You may assume that changing a culture of fear in, for example, your company or family isn't achievable. But we make culture every day, you and I and everyone, from what we tolerate and ignore, resist and reward. We are all making the soup we swim in.

In the next part of the book, we'll look at the biological reasons why we are all so primed for fear. And we'll discover techniques to boss that fear when it comes up at crucial times.

After that comes the deeper work: looking at all the different ways that distorted, *not-good-enough* fear behaviours show themselves. I'll share stories of people who've faced and overcome these, to give you ideas about what's happening in your head and how to change your story.

The book finishes with a manifesto – a summing up of everything I've presented. So once you've read the book, you'll be able to recap on the ideas quickly.

I hope you find your freedom in these pages.

A note on mental health

There's a line where the kind of fear that I'm talking about in this book, the kind that strains and drains our mental well-being, an everyday experience, can become something more.

Perhaps for you, as for millions of people all over the world, fear and anxiety do not just feel limiting but crippling. If your fear feels more like despair and endless blackness, you can't function and especially if you feel like you have suicidal thoughts, please know that this is a very real, very debilitating illness that needs care and support and healing from professionals and the people who love you.

It is never a good idea to deal with serious mental illness alone. If this is where you find yourself, you will find a list of resources in the back of this book to help guide you.

PART 1

Fear isn't just in your head and you're not alone

CHAPTER 1

Is your life a battlefield?

Where does fear come from? Everywhere.

Yes, fear comes from inside you: your mind, your beliefs, your thoughts. But an awful lot of it comes from outside you, from the culture as well as our environment.

This chapter is about all the messages, beliefs and accepted behaviours that you have absorbed from the culture but that are keeping you stuck in a fear mentality. I want to challenge these, help you see them clearly, so you don't have to be sucked into fear.

Human beings are the only species on the planet with an awareness that tomorrow we can be more than we are today. It might be this consciousness that marks us out. We spend our lives trying to improve and leave our old selves behind. You want to be better in future than you are today. And you want to be better than average at doing what matters most to you.

Your 'better' is personal. It might involve you taking your company public or your team winning the final. You could be gunning for a promotion, planning to get pregnant, wanting to buy a bigger house or run your first 5K.

Most of us go way beyond what's necessary. Striving at some level, grand or small, is human. And out of that comes our desire to win.

Of course, for some people and at some times, life can be a true fight for survival: physical, material or psychological survival. You have to dig deep for courage, face into your troubles and do the best you can with what you have. If this sounds like you, then I salute you.

However, for most of us in the Western world, our battles are largely man-made. We may be trying to beat a benchmark or target or the clock. Or our battleground might be a contest between teams or individuals at work or in sport. This type of fight isn't life-threatening, but gives us an insight into the 'battle narratives' that run our lives and underpin our social cultures.

Think about the language you use in everyday life. Do you talk about slaying it, killing it, nailing it? Or picking your battles, being armed with the facts, leading the charge, giving it a shot, bringing out the big guns, setting your sights on the prize, locked and loaded, rallying the troops, going ballistic? You get the idea.

In more masculinised cultures, such as in sport or the City or the legal world, you might encounter this kind of language as the norm. But that's true for both men and women who work in these kinds of competitive environments. If you're female, you might be more likely to use battle language on a more personal level: for example, I'm struggling to get the kids to sleep, I'm pinning someone down, fighting to get a moment to myself, dressed to kill, Beyoncé's use of 'slay'.

Our battle narratives have gone too deep. We have come to a point where many of us – maybe you – can only see life as a fight, a competition, even a war. It might feel like a battle to get the job you want, or get your kid out of the house in the morning, to negotiate traffic or the Tube, or the rudeness of strangers or the frustration of life admin. But is it useful to treat life as a fight?

While both men and women look at life in this way, it can play out slightly differently. The idea of fighting and physic-ally dominating each other is more likely to apply to men, but women also talk about fighting to get ahead, or staying on top to survive. The huge attention that goes into how women look is a form of competition, though increasingly men compete in that arena too. And both men and women compete for atten-tion, prestige and recognition.

A warrior is a combatant, trained for the field of war. Undoubtedly, a warrior spirit is a tremendous asset in compe-tition when it means being able to hold a single concentrated focus and find uncommon courage, unwavering endurance, clear thinking and composure under pressure. But with the deepest gratitude and respect for real warriors, I can't see why this is the right model for the rest of us to live by.

That model means that getting ahead, becoming unbeat-able and conquering other people are the primary motivators. It's not your fault: thinking of life as a battle has been drilled into us from a tender age, has lodged deep in our psyches. The myth that we need to dominate others in order to succeed our-selves has become our normal.

Do you belong to fight club?

A friend told me he'd just found a new hockey team for his seven-year-old son. It was six miles further to drive for practice, he said, but it would be worth it.

'What was wrong with the old team?' I asked.

'It was the coach, another dad,' he said. 'At half-time, they'd come off the pitch and he'd start on his pep talk. It was terrifying. He'd be all, "Keep on scrapping boys, keep going to the end. You're letting them get the better of you. You need to dominate them. We're here to win." They're seven, for goodness' sake.'

I can only assume that's how the coach was taught as a child. And I suspect that, like a lot of us, it's how he sees the wider world: as a battlefield, a place to dominate, compete. (There was a good ending, by the way. The coach in the new team gathered the boys in a huddle and talked about how they were here to have fun and do their best, to trust and believe in their own ability and in the team.)

Look back at your own life – perhaps back to your schooldays or even at home if you had siblings – and think about how often you were pitted against or compared to someone else: 'Your sister is the clever one'; 'You're not good enough for the first team'. As children, we can't help but take comparison on as a model of the world for ourselves.

You might be thinking that there's nothing wrong with competition. I want to do my best, to achieve, to succeed, to win. And not to be all, 'Oh you've got a prize for taking part'.

But think about this: have you taken this too far, too seriously? Is your desire to be better than everyone else, to win at all costs damaging you? That happens when, rather than coming out of a desire to see what you can achieve, it's coming out of your fear of failure, of losing out, of not being good enough. Or the flip side, you might be thinking of yourself as a loser before you even start, and therefore you don't want to compete at all.

Yes, there is huge value in competition, for its own sake and on the pitch. But not as a way of being. There is a chasm between wanting to be your best and wanting to be better than everyone else. And just because the default metaphor for our work, social and personal relationships has become the battlefield, that doesn't mean that we need to stick to that metaphor. As we'll see in forthcoming chapters, the language that we use shapes our experience of the world. In order to fear less, we need to reconfigure our world into a much kinder and more accepting one than a field of battle.

CHAPTER 2

What kind of winning are you doing?

What is your definition of success? Have you ever got what you wanted, but then found yourself unsatisfied, wanting more? This chapter is about why this happens, which I call *winning shallow*. And about how to get the opposite into your life: real fulfilment, which I call *winning deep*.

One elite player I worked with, Paul, offers a perfect illustration of what winning shallow looks like. As with most of the people whose stories come from my professional life, I've disguised Paul's identity to protect him, not least because he spoke to me in trust. But the essence of what he and the others share – the sentiments and emotions they express – are very real.

If you've ever dreamed of being a sports star, and imagined how incredible it would be to be at the very top of your game, Paul's account may surprise you. Especially since, as he told me, he'd wanted to play football since the age of five. It should have been his dream come true.

He remembered sitting with his grandad in a small room in suburbia, watching the cup final. His team sealed the result with a devastating last-minute strike. He could still describe its exact angle and trajectory. That was when he told his grandad that he was going to be the best player the club had ever seen: one day he was going to hold up that trophy.

As well as deep desire, Paul had talent. As it took shape and he matured physically, he lost himself for hours with the ball at his feet in the back streets, involved in the dramas and plots, glorious victories and shock defeats with his best mates. I asked him how he'd describe playing at that time. His answer was simple: 'It felt great.'

The best part of his week as a teenager was training. He revelled in the coaches' feedback and lessons. A natural show-off, he loved to impress with his skills and make other people smile with his tricks and antics. He described the pride he felt when his coach told him he was being scouted by a big-name club, running home from training dizzy with excitement, 'as if I was on stilts'.

His professional career lasted a respectable 15 years, until he was 29. Sadly, that moment of being scouted was the pinnacle of his happiness in the game.

It was when he moved into the senior team, a relatively late debutante aged 20, that he started to notice 'the slide'.

'I thought this was just how it must be with the big boys. It was harder. I don't mean physically, I have always been willing to put in physically, but it was harsher too. Within a few years of getting my first game and buzzing about it, my excitement about making the team had worn off. The play had gone out of playing. Everything got serious. People kept telling me to keep my head down and focus, that other lads would kill to have my opportunities, and I should be grateful. Well, I was grateful, but also sort of disappointed. And I couldn't say anything. How could I admit I didn't feel good when everyone else thinks you're living the dream?

'I had a few injuries, usually minor. But one year, I had a hip injury that kept me out for almost a season. I had to do a lot of time on the bikes and in the pool in recovery, away from the other boys. No one likes recovery as it's as boring as hell, but you have to do it. The coach wasn't much of a talker. But it still pisses me off that the only thing he said to me in those months was: "Plenty of young talent after your shirt, lad, and they are all better than you."

'The lads laughed that off with a jab to the ribs and a bit of banter. And, as you do, I laughed along with them and played it like "big man, don't care". But I felt really bad. It took me a long time to admit I was hurt. I was worried because I could see all the lads progressing. It started to eat me up.

'My first game back, I was so anxious about mucking it up. From then on, I was always trying to prove myself, so serious. Most of the time, my hip was killing me but I said nothing. Then about six weeks back in, in the middle of a game, I felt something click in my hip and I dropped in pain. I wish I'd stayed on my feet, however bad the pain. As I came off, I heard the coach say "weak" or something like that. I felt embarrassed but also sad and angry. I decided I'd fucking show him I wasn't weak.

'The doc said I'd need surgery but it could wait. So for the rest of the season I had a series of let's just say "not-very-nice" weekly injections in my hip so I could play. In training, I gritted it out. I never said a word about the pain to anyone but the doc.

'When I look back, I can see I wasn't very nice to the people around me, especially my wife. I drifted from the boys. I felt numb and cold. I felt like a piece of meat being processed. I just turned off and did my job. I thought, maybe this is what you have to do to win. I didn't even talk to my grandad about any of it. He still thought footy was the be-all-and-end-all.

'That same year, we won the final. And I got to lift that trophy. I remember being in the changing room after the game and looking at a sign on the wall that said, "there is no finish line". I thought, "I wish there fucking was." Everyone was cracking beers and carrying on, all smiles and singing, I joined in but all I felt was empty. I didn't even feel like me any more. Maybe I was a bit depressed, maybe I'm just soft, or maybe I am "weak".

'Someone asked me recently if I wanted my kid to play. Not really. I don't want to see his spark put out.'

Paul's career is a classic case of winning shallow. His joy in playing – and eventually in life – was extinguished by the fear-mongering culture of his club.

Could you be winning shallow? Often, the clue is that you feel burned out, like Paul. Do you sense you've lost your excitement or joy in life? Bored? As if you're going through the motions? Maybe you used to take huge pleasure in playing sport or another activity, but that's gone?

Let's dig deeper to see why this might have happened.

We lose our way when our lives are underpinned by either wanting to be better than others or wanting to avoid being rejected by others. There are two parts to wanting to be better than others, and you may recognise them both.

Always wanting more

The first question to ask yourself is: do you think about success in terms of upward gains, continually acquiring more and doing better?

This happens naturally; consciously and unconsciously we rank ourselves and others according to our external achievements. It might be a blatant status symbol: what car do you drive? What's your house worth? Where do you live? What's your job title? What do you do for work? Or a subtle one: what grades did your kid get? Cornwall or Croatia? Where did you go to university? H&M or Harrods?

This kind of one-upmanship has its most recent roots in the eighties, when the idea emerged that what we have is more important than who we are. The trouble is, if you use that ranking, what you have can never be enough. So Paul achieved the ultimate success of making the first team. But when he got there, and even when his team lifted the trophy, he didn't feel the joy he'd expected. He was constantly told that he was lucky to get to where he was, that the other lads were better than him, and that culture took root in his mind. Fear had left him anxious and isolated.

Fear uses up all the space we might have for broader, less gain-oriented ambitions: maybe you would have loved to have played the piano more, or learned to skateboard, or become a painter rather than an accountant?

The school system feeds into this: we are most often marked on academic results, rather than the broader qualities that might help us find real fulfilment. No child takes a GCSE in becoming a compassionate friend or being more creative or having great ideas. The focus is almost exclusively on exam results.

It really shouldn't be. The human psyche is an ecosystem that thrives when it is rich and diverse, not driven towards constant upgrades. If you are always trying to reach and demonstrate success, you are missing out on the journey, on experiencing yourself and others and exploring the world.

Think about this: how much of your attention and mind is consumed with looking good enough, with making it seem like you're OK in everybody else's eyes? Perhaps you may think of yourself as too cool to keep up with the Joneses, but isn't being cool just another way to measure yourself? And is comparison really what you want to spend your precious energy on? Are you leaving any room for who else you might be?

On the flip side, maybe you tell yourself you're a failure or a loser because you haven't achieved the status markers: the relationship, the house, the career, the baby. I've seen this happen to even the most glamorous, accomplished and high-status people: there's always someone who can trump you, with a bigger or better car or house or any other of our culture's thousands of status symbols.

If she wins, I'm a loser

The second question to ask yourself is: do you feel that if someone else wins, you are more likely to lose? Believing that success is scarce and limited makes you want to be better than the next person, to think you have to fight tooth and nail for success.

Say a competitor enters your market. Do you analyse what they're doing well and learn from it? Or do you go all out to crush them? The same thing can happen on a personal level, too: creating friction with colleagues because they feel like competition.

In ecology, scarcity is about getting base survival needs met even at the expense of others. In humans, scarcity is also psychology; it is the ego's need to be better than the next guy and the fear of not having or being enough.

The scarcity mentality says there isn't enough winning to go around, not enough opportunity, possibility, time, talent, competence, admiration, resource, success, wealth, love or joy. So you'd better get yours quick before someone else does, make sure that the next guy doesn't get a bite of your slice.

You'll know you're in a scarcity mentality when you can only think of yourself and your own interests, or those of your tribe (the people you see as like you in some way). Without realising it, that scarcity-scrap to *be good enough* and to *have enough* can shape your mentality into one of dominance, self-focus and must-conquer.

This drive to dominate doesn't necessarily slow down, even once you bank some gains. In fact, like Paul, you may feel a greater sense of scarcity once you have more to lose. This may also include your reputation as a winner!

In your mind it might not feel enough just to win: you want to smash, outstrip, out-run, squash and annihilate any possibility that you are not good enough, to prove beyond doubt that you are not a loser and get yourself on to safe ground. Something shifts: it's not that you want to win, it's that you cannot afford to lose. A scarcity mentality never lets you feel on safe ground. It turns a desire to win from being good for the soul and a product of us at our best into a neurotic, desperate, and pretty ugly need.

And when you go from desire to need, the underlying reason is fear.

Many people believe having this kind of desperation is a good motivator. That's how Paul's coach operated. And it explains these 'motivational' mantras: 'No rest', 'Be afraid', 'There is no finish line'.

By contrast, consider the New Zealand All Blacks, arguably the world's greatest team in any sport. The All Blacks player Brad Thorn has a simple mantra: 'Champions do extra'. Can you feel a profoundly different tone? That is the difference between fear and desire.

Having a scarcity mentality reduces the game of life to black or white, good or bad, winner or loser. When winning itself is also reduced to one ultra-specific goal, such as winning a World Cup, beating a commercial competitor or getting a dream job, it's winning shallow. And not winning means being a failure. Then, it doesn't take long for the soul and purpose to be squashed out of winning altogether, replaced by the fear of being that failure.

You may have all the trophies in the cabinet or all the gold stars on your résumé, but unless you can take the reins back from fear, you cannot win deep.

Winning doesn't have to come with fear. Winning deep feels completely and utterly different. Imagine this: success that has nothing to do with your worth as a person and everything to do with the joy of getting to know yourself as a human being. You'd no longer see winning in terms of a war with yourself and everyone else. You could cultivate a mentality that's about expansion and experience and connection to others, not dominance and gain. How much further might you go, and how different might it feel?

Winning can feel particularly rewarding when there is a big risk that you might lose or fail. Remember when you had to hold your nerve and manage your emotions, maybe fend off doubters, drill down into resources you weren't sure you had? In comparison, success that comes easily feels bland and faded. (That's why we all hate cheating so much; it sucks out the rewards.)

Winning like this can be intense, contagious, can flood the soul of the winner with joy. Just listen to Andy Ruiz Jr., the Mexican-American world heavyweight boxing champion who, in 2019, knocked out Anthony Joshua in the seventh round, delivering one of boxing's greatest upsets:

> This is what I've been dreaming about, this is what I have been working hard for and I can't believe I just made my dreams come true. It's a blessing man, you know what I'm still pinching myself to see if this is true. All that hard work and dedication that we did in the gym, the praying, I just followed my dreams and I made them come true . . . this is what I've been working for my whole life . . . I'm the first Mexican heavyweight champion of the world!
>
> Andy Ruiz Jr ringside after Ruiz Jr. vs. Joshua, 2019

Or, if you want to know what winning deep looks and feels like in the long term, TV host, producer, best-selling author and traveller Leon Logothetis, presenter of Netflix show *The Kindness Diaries*, is a great example. He used to be an unhappy and depressed stockbroker, who gave it up to travel around the world. So far, he's visited over 90 countries, in each one relying on the kindness of the strangers he meets for a room and food. But in his new show, he's giving back too, in the form of money to people who are doing good deeds. 'My favourite type of person is a person who comes from their heart,' he says.

He's winning deep because he has decided what success looks like in his life, rather than someone else's version, the financial success that was leaving him empty. And also because he's breaking down the lazy 'that's just the way it is' stereotypes that insist the only way to get on is by thinking of the world as dog-eat-dog. Finally, he's winning deep because his wins are focused beyond himself on seeing and growing kindness; his success is all about connecting with others in common humanity.

Winning deep is more satisfying and realistic, and ultimately closer to unlocking our deepest potential. Because it comes from the heart, mind and soul, it stops you seeing your potential as something you might miss out on, and instead you see it as vast, untapped and available. It allows you to compete and create until you have nothing left in your bones to give. And it means you'll fear less.

CHAPTER 3

What are your beliefs about success?

Along with assuming that we need to be better than the next person in order to succeed, there are a whole host of other winning myths we absorb from our culture. All the cultures we live in – our family, team, group, company, our nations and our global culture – teach us what it means to win and what it will take. The trouble is a lot of them simply promote more fear.

If you were fortunate, you may have absorbed positive and useful lessons about winning and success from your family, friends, school, college, work and nation. But it's likely you will also have picked up some fear-promoting beliefs. This chapter spells out some those I've come across most often, so you can ask if they're really serving you well.

Success myth 1: Losing turns you into a loser

As human beings, we are fascinated by accomplishment: what can emerge from our muscles, pumps, levers, brain cells and nerve tissue. We are awed by extraordinary human feats, so much so that they can bond a whole nation while they inspire us individually to push for excellence.

Maybe you pulled out your trainers and hit the pavement after watching an incredible achievement on the track (I know I did after watching Mo Farah at the London Olympics). Or perhaps you picked up the guitar again after being moved by a blindingly good concert.

We especially love to see accomplishment when it's unexpected. That's the premise for hit TV programmes like *The X Factor* and *The Voice*. The set-up starts with how unassuming the unknown performer is, or shows us the adversity they have faced. And then they step on stage, open their mouth, and beauty flows out.

It's likely you learned that a never-ending pursuit of your potential is good, too. That you should want to be faster, go higher, get stronger and be smarter. It could be practical: how to make your begonias bloom better this year or trying to improve your stamina enough to get a violin solo. It could be emotional: attempting to understand your partner's perspective when you disagree. It could be mental: wanting to speak up confidently in class.

But there's a flip side to this positive message: you need to be afraid of losing.

Looked at logically, this is ridiculous. We can all see that to become a winner, at some point you have to lose. The existence of the eternal winner is a romanticised myth. People may make success look effortless, but it rarely is. The actress Jessica Chastain spent four years in Los Angeles, going to free yoga classes because she didn't have any money, before she landed her first audition. Larry David spent a year in his late thirties writing for *Saturday Night Live*, but only one of his sketches was aired. Then he joined up with Jerry Seinfeld to create the eponymous show. The story of J.K. Rowling's first Harry Potter manuscript being rejected by 12 publishers has achieved legendary status.

Success comes from trying, extending yourself and taking risks, which means that inevitably, you will fail along the way. And you will fail often. Yes: every day of your life you'll win some and lose some.

Losing takes all kinds of forms. At work, you might have missed out on a promotion or just misspelt the CEO's name. At college, you could have bombed an exam or left out one test question. On a dating app, you spent hours but didn't match with one person, or you found out your new partner was seeing other people.

The scale doesn't matter. What does matter is your will to excavate the failure, reassess, rethink and move forward – maybe in a new direction.

If you do this, failing becomes valuable. Because it allows you to learn where you are not yet ready or skilled enough. It might not be easy or pleasant, but you can make it useful.

The best attitude to failure is the one that willingly invites it. When sports teams analyse games on video, a good coach doesn't say: 'There, that is where you mucked up.' They say: 'What do you see here? Tell me what was going on for you out there? What do you think caused the error? What will help you for next time this comes up?'

The direct experience that comes from trying and failing is the key to solving future problems and overcoming barriers. And it's way more effective than hanging around, hoping that no problems or barriers arise. The earlier you fail, the more often you fail and the braver you are about it, the more you're protected from losing the plot when the biggest moments come.

We aren't taught this. The message we get is that failing or losing equals not being good enough as a human being. We think if we fail, we are worth less.

That is when fear comes in and crowds out your mind. If you believe losing makes you a loser, you are so much more likely to avoid trying at all. You may have done this: sabotaged yourself so you failed earlier on when the stakes are low – rather than be exposed as a loser later on. Or you may have made excuses for why you can't try right now: 'I'm too busy'; 'I can't afford to take the risk of leaving my job.' Inside, you will know if saying these things – or your own version – is a true reason or an excuse.

Really, you shouldn't see failure as part of you, but just as giving you a puzzle to solve.

Yet that's not the message most of us absorb. We let failure leave behind a smear on our character, rather than simply being an indicator of our performance on a given day. And that makes us reluctant to show imperfection or vulnerability, in case it's mistaken for weakness.

The truth? Losing is for winners.

Success myth 2: Fear is the best motivator

We have all learned that fear is a necessary tool to motivate someone else to succeed. And that without it, people often won't bother.

It's true that fear is one of the most powerful motivators in a crisis; it's not a myth that people find superhuman strength in a moment of danger, for example, lifting a car if someone is trapped underneath. You will have heard of the adventurer Aron Ralston, who ended up with his arm trapped by a boulder during a solo canyoneering trip in the wilds of Utah. Five days later, with no other way of getting free, he broke two of his arm bones, then cut off the arm with the penknife on a multi-use tool. Here, the fear of death spurred him on to do something intensely painful, but necessary in order to give him the greatest chance of survival.

And if you know there will be an unwanted consequence for not performing – getting dropped from your team or missing out on something you care about – then you naturally up your game.

But do you *really* need to be scared in order to succeed? It's fair to say that some people in authority are scarier than others. So we make sure we don't cross them, either by doing what they want or avoiding being noticed by them.

There's a huge gulf between being respected and inspiring fear. I had a basketball coach who, if you made a mistake, said nothing. A look was enough to make me focus. But he wasn't a bully; his composure and presence inspired me to be better because I didn't want to disappoint him. This is not such a bad way to keep your charges on track. This approach is along the lines of the Pep Guardiola or Gregg Popovich school of coaching: they don't have to say much for their presence to be felt.

But inspiring fear in order to get results or to motivate someone is different. It's deliberate intimidation.

You might have had a teacher or even a parent who ruled by intimidation, who made you feel small or humiliated. Roald Dahl specialised in creating monstrous characters in this vein: the aunts in *James and the Giant Peach*, for example, and Miss Trunchbull in *Matilda*. Or if you've seen the 2014 movie *Whiplash* about a young jazz drummer training at a music conservatory, his ruthless instructor and conductor is the prime example of an authoritarian teacher ruling by fear. Not only does the instructor repeatedly humiliate students by insulting both their playing and their personalities, but he also manipulates them by giving and taking away the coveted position of core drummer in the band, including pitting them against each other in a brutal five-hour audition.

Hollywood loves a fear story. One kind is the boss in *The Devil Wears Prada*, monstrous in the demands she puts on her assistants and such a tyrant that nobody will even get in the lift with her. Or Jason Bourne, who achieves impossible feats because he's fuelled by adrenalin and fear.

In real life, constant fear is simply too exhausting and distracting to be a good motivator. That's because your attention is finite, and the more attention you spend worrying about scary negative consequences, the less attention you have to give to your actual performance. If you are playing for your place on the team, you are not focused on playing to win.

And although we react quickly to fear motivations, we also react in pretty limited ways. Fear tends to lead to more fear, which leads to insularity as well as us-and-them thinking.

This doesn't have to be the case. One great example of uniting people in the face of fear is the leadership shown by Jacinda Ardern, the prime minister of New Zealand. This is part of the beautiful speech she made at the memorial service for the Christchurch mosques attacks:

> Because we are not immune to the viruses of hate, of fear, of other. We never have been. But we can be the nation that discovers the cure. And so to each of us as we go from here, we have work to do, but do not leave the job of combatting hate to the government alone. We each hold the power, in our words and in our actions, in our daily acts of kindness. Let that be the legacy of the fifteenth of March. To be the nation we believe ourselves to be.

Her compassion and strength in the face of terrorism on home soil motivated people to react with humanity, not just fear. Not all of the 'motivational' fear you'll experience exists in plain sight. Withdrawal, exclusion and silence are classic passive-aggressive techniques of intimidation. As this kind is not so obvious, you may have to detect it from your own fear response, or simply from the fact you feel rubbish when you are around a particular person. It might be your boss not answering your question, dismissing or ignoring you, or a not-so-secret glance between other people when you speak, the kind that lets you know you're being judged.

In fact, manipulating with fear is a lazy way to motivate. I can't see any results that couldn't be achieved with better skills and more care. Once introduced, fear doesn't stay specific but reproduces and spreads. It lodges in our mentality like termites in redwood. A fear-based environment leaves little room for enthusiasm, excitement, imagination or the rising sense of possibility.

Success myth 3: Only the fittest survive

This phrase 'survival of the fittest' has become shorthand for the idea that the most brutally competitive individuals, organisations and institutions, those with the most aggressive and exclusionary traits, will win. It's the ethos of Jordan Belfort, the Wolf of Wall Street: 'My warriors, who won't take "No" for an answer. Who won't hang up the phone till their client either buys. Or fucking dies!'

What's interesting is that this dog-eat-dog or eat-or-be-eaten version of winning, which I'd say is the essence of winning shallow, is based on a false assumption. Survival of the fittest is a misunderstood and misused phrase.

The term was coined by a philosopher and economist called Herbert Spencer in 1864 after reading Charles Darwin's brilliant theory of natural selection in *On the Origin of Species*. You might assume – and this is down to Spencer's interpretation of Darwin's theory – that 'survival of the fittest' means one animal's ability to conquer another. What Spencer did was combine Darwin's biological theory with his economic theories and come out with Social Darwinism, the stretched, sketchy idea that there are favoured races and types of people in life's struggle. His use of the theory suggested that human beings had evolved to become the ordained rulers of the earth. And the ones who made it to powerful positions (largely white middle-class men doing so by force), did so because they were naturally selected and thus the 'fittest' for the job. The idea of Social Darwinism has been deployed in service of class struggles, war, racism and the pursuit of trophies.

What Darwin actually wrote was far more nuanced. It's also a useful way you could think about the world. Boiling it down, what he said is that the form of a species that will survive into future generations is the one that makes the most reproductive copies of itself. So being the fittest was about effective breeding, not strength or the ability to beat others and sit at the top of the food chain.

Many species find creative and almost unimaginable ways to reproduce and beat the odds without needing to dominate. Male cichlids in Lake Tanganyika in eastern Africa gather to release a huge cloud of sperm; the females release their eggs into it, then incubate the fertilised eggs in their mouths. A male clownfish is able to change sex when the dominant female dies. Survival of the fittest, you could say, is as much about being a lover as a fighter.

Later, Darwin expanded his ideas further to say that survival isn't just down to being the best at breeding, but also at adapting to the local environment. And adaptation comes from cooperation, collaboration, becoming resilient to change and making the most of opportunities, not just dominating. It's these qualities, not power or dominance, that are the key to your potential.

Look at the people in your own life who are real winners, who've really excelled or grown in some way. What is it about them that has helped them succeed? You won't see an overarching need to crush competitors. Instead, you're likely to identify that they're creative, innovative, willing to change, move on and let go. They are able to build good energy in communities, collaborate and exchange ideas. And you'll see plenty of diversity – of thoughts, experiences and tactics – as well as the power to resist doubt.

Those are the real 'fittest', the people who are worth learning from.

Success myth 4: If you're not in, you're out

There was a popular T-shirt that some of us 'jocks' wore at university. It said: 'it's not the winning, it's the taking *apart*'. I was so proud of that T-shirt. It was a badge of belonging to a group that back then I saw as superior and important.

Belonging is a deep human need. Have you ever noticed you've unconsciously changed your accent to sound more like the person you're speaking to? Because of our fear of being rejected, most of us unthinkingly adapt to the group.

In evolutionary terms, being in the tribe is what keeps us safe and protected. It also gives us a clear identity and rules to navigate life: when you belong, you take on the social values and responsibilities of the group. That's true whether you're in cricket's Barmy Army or Extinction Rebellion. At its best, belonging looks like a strong sense of community or pride in the group, both good for mental and physical well-being.

But where competition of some kind comes into the picture, belonging can turn into tribal loyalty. It isn't necessarily bad to take pride in your group or team and have a strong identity that you want to share and shout about. In fact, it's a wonderful feeling when you're part of a common experience, whether you're on the Moon Walk for breast cancer, or marching against Brexit. This is particularly true when what you're doing lifts other people's spirits.

So tribalism isn't all bad. In fact, it can have something of a sacred quality when it ensures your best efforts to deserve your membership. That goes for any elite team, from the England football team and the Golden State Warriors to the Royal Marines.

The issue with tribalism is th
into exclusion and elitism. So you're
yours, it's us or them. This kind of 'peo
is about being superior, better than. Fo
example, can be funny, inspirational, uplif
coming home'), or they can be nasty, pers
oted. Take England's 2019 victory over Bulgar
when the match had to be stopped twice because
with Bulgarian fans doing vile monkey chants an
salutes.

A tribe can be around an idea or concept — such
politics — as much as a physical group, but in the extrem
the bottom line is that the tribe is right, better and exclusive. The British class system is a masterclass in tribalism,
as is politics. In fact, in exclusive tribes anywhere, there's a
narrow view of what's right. The group aim is often to
dominate, to conquer, to have status and to position yourself above others. And outsiders are seen as less than tribe
members.

If we believe we need to be in the tribe, to belong to the
special group at any cost, it makes us scared that we might
one day be excluded. If we believe membership is hard to
come by, it puts us into a scarcity mentality. If we're in a
group that excludes others, it disconnects us from them. And
it ups the likelihood of conflict with other groups: for example,
how even now conversations around Brexit can feel divisive
and sensitive. Or the way Twitter can blow up into a polar-
ised debate.

It might feel safe and even good to be on the inside of a
group. But think about this: what are you compromising on in
order to belong?

...itish sporting insti-
... that reads, 'Logic
... half of yourself

...ry discipline
... in critical

...best and only way
...or, so must be contained

...ow how to keep a cool head when under
...ing our plane', the term given to this skill by Dr
...ired, the elite performance coach. We all benefit from
using logic to tame anxiety in critical moments (indeed this
has been a key part of my work and I'll be writing about how
to do it in chapter 7). It's a skill that any person who performs
under pressure needs to learn.

But should we always be living as if every moment is
critical?

Absolutely not. Reducing human beings to logical, invul-
nerable and robotic performers on a pressing timeline goes
against how we work. It undermines our potential, and indeed
provokes performance anxiety.

It is a rare bird who can get more out of themselves over the
long term when they are relentlessly pushing with no reprieve
than when they are filled with passion, purpose and a sense of
identity. If you push yourself that hard and it feels fine to you, it's
worth asking how the people around you are experiencing your
drive. You might find they are dying to get out of your way.

Success myth 6: You need to sacrifice

This is one for the workaholics. It says that you should compromise pretty much everything else in your life for the sake of success. It says you need to be hyper-individual and take on hyper-masculine qualities. And it says performance is such a grave and serious struggle that it requires 100 percent vigilance, seriousness and a sense of everlasting urgency.

I remember, earlier in my career, listening to a coach making a speech along these lines. As he spoke the words, he came across as burned out, desperate in his need to conquer.

> We can't afford to be all love and smooches and all
> of that fluff. This is a fight, a struggle to the death
> and if you're not up for it, you can get out. You need
> to understand that it's dog-eat-dog. This is war and
> there can be no surrender. It's not for the faint-
> hearted. It's for the few not the many, for champions
> only.

You can't help being practically struck in the face by the machismo. But also by the limitations of what he's saying. This is a black-or-white way of being: you're either a sledge-hammer or a failure. None of your other skills, talents and traits — imagination, creativity, humour, composure, adaptability or patience — are worth bringing to the party.

Sadly, this hasn't been unusual either in elite sport or in any area where personal gain or glory is up for grabs. Recently, a colleague shared with me a conversation that he'd had with a high-level coach:

I'm a selfish bastard and I'm prepared to compromise
everything to get what I want. I am ruthless about this.
When I look back on what I sacrificed, how much I
hurt, what I lost out on, you would think I might care.
My family knows the deal. It didn't and doesn't mean
anything to me. I would do it all again to get the
chance at winning. It's a privilege.

Does this sound pathological to anyone else? Does this sound
like striving for our best as human beings, or a bucket full of
anger, resentment and fear?

The belief that comes along with the struggle myth is that
you need to wait until after work and/or performance to enjoy
yourself, to hang out with family, to have loving relationships,
to prioritise your well-being or to invest in community or
causes.

This urgent-struggle belief is familiar to many of us. You
feel you need to make it through the next challenge – that
day, that competition, that degree, that child's schooling –
before you can put more time into the people you love. You
can even hold this belief on behalf of your children; just think
of the so-called Tiger Parents who fill their children's time
with achievements and activities.

Oh, and 'putting time into' isn't just about being in the
room. It's about being wholly present mentally and spiritually.
That means being truly with them, without the nagging urge
to check your emails in pursuit of not getting left behind.

There's often a second part to this. It's that you have a
perfect-seeming public self for work, and a private one where
you take off the mask. And you'd hate to let your colleagues
see the real, flawed you.

But the more you're run by the fear of not succeeding, the less of your real self you feel you can expose. Ask yourself: what would you lose if you *did* reveal the sides of you that are less polished, less conformist, less 'perfect', less strong? What if you showed you could be more individual, more curious, and perhaps more fun?

You might feel you'd run the risk of being seen as not committed or not hungry enough. That's hardly surprising: at work and in sport we're often judged on whether we are giving 110 percent. When was the last time you heard someone say, 'I don't really think that he goofed off and laughed enough' or 'He would have gone further if he was less serious about his grades'? Maybe never.

Instead of giving half of your precious energy to avoiding being exposed, or to fear of failure, wouldn't it be great to simply know deep in your heart that you will be fine? Because you *are* fine, just as you are.

Your fear-promoting beliefs

Which of the six success myths do you subscribe to? Some of them may interweave and overlap. Hopefully you can now see how they're built on fear, and how they perpetuate fear.

You may be quite attached to one or two of these beliefs – they've got you this far, after all – so they could be difficult to shed. But perhaps you can at least accept they might not be fundamental truths. They've been sold to us, and they are only adding fear to our lives.

CHAPTER 4

Is your environment fear-full?

All of the fear-filled beliefs about success – that we need to beat, conquer, struggle with and fight each other for it – have infected our daily environments too. That often means the workplace, but it could refer to any group, even your family.

So how do you know if you're in a toxic fear-filled company, team or institution? One sign is that you just don't feel right, and regularly run into conflict and negativity. The cause of your dis-ease may well be the level of unspoken fear underlying your day-to-day interactions, causing you unconscious distress that you don't feel that you can show or name.

Of course, some environments are more overtly toxic than others. Where there is extreme bullying, not least in places online that are thick with resentment and ugly commentary, you'll see people baiting using fear and shame. You can see it in playgrounds, sports grounds, workplaces and boardrooms, and it's a staple on screen, too. Think *Mean Girls*: 'You can't sit with us!'

There are more subtle shades of bullying, intimidation and baiting. These insidious, often unseen exchanges can create confusion and wear you down mentally. The stealthy bully might look fine to everyone else, so you start to doubt yourself. But bullying always strips away well-being layer by layer.

You likely won't want to say anything. Human beings have an unbelievable ability to adapt or fit in in order to avoid being singled out. We'll do whatever we need to, however far away from our comfort zone it takes us, however miserable the bullying makes us. You could say we're chameleons but there's a more apt animal: the Indonesian mimic octopus. Not only can it change colour, texture, shape and behaviour but it can impersonate other species, from anemones and lion fish to jellyfish and sea snakes.

In toxic environments, shame is often used as the guard dog for conforming. Even while your self-image is suffering, you might assume things are OK if you look good on the out-side. You may not even realise how far you have moulded yourself to suit an environment that stirs up your fear. Often nobody else mentions it either because they've adapted just like you have.

You're also likely to have got used to it. Maybe you're gen-erally good at coping, the sort of person who doesn't get their feathers ruffled easily. And you're fine in the rest of your life.

The more your environment is infused with fear, the more you will respond to life negatively. You may not be able to make a direct and causal connection to why you feel a bit funky and agitated; perhaps no one 'said' or 'did' anything obvious, but you'll regularly feel tense without being able to explain why.

But be assured, it's not in your own head. We take fear in from our environments like a thirsty plant sucking up water.

For example, perhaps there's a particular colleague who stands out for you. In your regular Monday morning meeting, they might not say anything overtly aggressive. But their body language betrays them – arms crossed, looking away when you speak. This prompts you to become vigilant, makes you think, 'I'd better not get anything wrong.' And, boom! You're in a fear trap.

It's exhausting to live like this. It's as if sandpaper is constantly scraping off the top from your comfort.

Fear is most often found in environments that promote old-school, suck-it-up toughness, and use threat and shame as motivational tools. The following are some of the red flags that show the system you're operating in is faulty.

1. It's passive-aggressive

Passive-aggressive leaders don't quite say what they mean – which would allow you to respond directly – but they give enough fear-breeding, non-verbal and half-masked clues to tell you that losing or failing would be deadly. It might be something along the lines of, 'Well if you don't feel you are up to it at the moment, we can look to down-size your role and give it to someone who is.' One executive described a five-year dysfunctional relationship with a passive-aggressive boss like this: 'It wasn't what she said. It was the withering look and the pause and sigh before speaking that left me with the feeling I'd disappointed her, yet again. It was only when I left that I real-ised I'd spent all that time afraid of not pleasing her.'

I have also seen employees unofficially placed in what one well-known company calls 'the Hawaii suite', the work ver-sion of sending someone to Coventry. This churns over the fear that lives inside all of us, exposing more of it – fear-raking, if you like. In the Hawaii suite, the person is intentionally excluded from the conversations they need to be in to function well, but they still have performance expectations. Because no one says anything upfront or out loud, they are left marooned and second-guessing.

Another common workplace fear-raker is getting mixed messages. That's when you're told your work isn't strong enough but, with no other input, you're left doing the same job. Or you're told you're playing well but you're then deselected.

Both passive-aggression and a deliberate lack of clarity are the very opposite of the straight-shooting, open-hearted feed-back culture that helps performance.

2. It's predatory

This environment is deeply competitive, so someone has to lose. You feel like prey, as if you could be a target, that the predators are ready for you to make a mistake. So you have to get things right all the time – there's no room for error.

You also have to meet the performance standard or you're out, or at least singled out. This can be obvious – a sales job where you have to make your target to get a bonus. It can be less overt too; for example, you desperately want to avoid being publicly seen as failing or not 'getting it'. Or you don't want the fact you're behind deadline to be broadcast in a team meeting. In predatory environments, there's often an element of public humiliation.

The aggression may be less obvious, for example, if mocking or teasing are normal ways of communicating. This can happen in families too, where you have to watch what you say or do, because someone is going to be the butt of the joke. People might say teasing is a just a bit of fun, and it might be delivered with a smile and a smack on the back, but it's always looking for a victim. And whether it's you being picked on or not, the feeling you're left with is: 'is it my turn next?'

No matter if the aggression is obvious or hidden, it keeps you emotionally malnourished and it keeps feeding your cortisol levels. It also pushes you into fear habits. For example, you might give yourself a do-or-die message: 'I can't lose this one' or 'I have to pass this test' or 'this will be a disaster' or 'I have to do this one perfectly' or 'I cannot let there be one single complaint this time or else'. Even if you make such statements half-jokingly, without a second thought, you and those around you will start to feel the weight of it.

3. It's power-based

In high-control organisations and institutions, there's a welded-on power structure. Those at the top make the decisions, the rest have to follow the rules.

You'll likely feel uneasy making suggestions that might be considered off topic and off brand. You can't challenge the existing plans. You might receive feedback such as, 'This sounds a bit loose' or 'Show me where this has worked previously'. Or my personal favourite, 'This is too horoscopey', which means unscientific, unproven, and therefore invalid.

What this creates is a veil of control, so you make sure you don't do anything that might be judged as stupid. Or worse, as 'not aligned with us'. Just sharing a thought can feel like a formal performance. In meetings in high-control organisations, you might carefully avoid being too personal. You'll make sure you're presenting your ideas in a structured, conforming and data-reliant style. And you'll shut down your imagination, stop thinking about what's possible or could be improved or changed, as it'll feel too scary to be in any way controversial.

There are other ways of being over-controlling, for example, managers who don't trust people to get the work done. Their fear is that if people are given even an inch of freedom, they will slack off. This kind of company struggles with letting people have flexi-time or home-working. It's often where you'll find a culture of 'presenteeism', where staff sit at their desks and stare at their screens, present but not really there.

In these sorts of organisations, you have to fit in, not stand out. You comply, not defy. You are also supposed to 'stay in your lane' rather than stray over into anyone else's area with ideas or imagination. In systems like this, the central energy is anxiety and you end up paying far too much mental rent.

4. It's possessive

There's a difference between feeling a part of a company, an institution, a team or a school and feeling owned. Too much control over what a person does or says and how a person acts can start to feel possessive. 'Our people', 'Our students', 'Our team' . . . on 'Our terms', for 'Our benefit'. Do you have to give too much to belong?

In this kind of organisation, you may feel you're being treated like a robot, or a cog in a machine. It's as if human beings are just a component part of the system rather than the point of the system, as if we are merely results-maximisers focused on gaining a competitive advantage.

It may feel as if you have sold your soul for a price decided by HR. The vibe you get is that you should be grateful to work for this company, to have this job. And you'd better swallow the values and the norms wholesale, because if you want to think differently, you're in trouble. If this is your family vibe, there might be a matriarch or patriarch who – overtly or by stealth – overinfluences the other family members' lives. In a team, you might absorb the idea that you are lucky to play for them, so you should shut up and be grateful.

An acquaintance recently told me about a new team coach who was absolutely insistent he wouldn't select a player with dreadlocks. The coach said it looked 'sloppy' and he wanted his players to look professional. Not only is this culturally unconscious, it screams of power and ownership. It says, 'you'd better look and feel like me, or else'. Even if the players were to conform, something would be for ever sanitised in the player–coach relationship; the personal is lost. And performance is nothing if not personal. (That coach didn't last, by the way.)

There is a poverty that comes from insisting on uniformity. Something beautiful is lost when you try to control people's individuality, make everything and everyone the same shape and size culturally and in their character.

So what if a kid wants to wear his shirt differently, or she wants to shave the side of her head? So what if a player wants one sock up and one sock down during a game, or a gymnast wants to wear a mohawk?

Why do we feel the need to wear shirts and ties that project faceless similarity and conformity? What would happen if you came to work as *you*? Would it mean you were less hidden, more exposed? Would it be scary to just be yourself?

Living and working in fear

None of these overly controlling, fear-based environments are places where you can bud, then blossom. Instead, you feel like you constantly need to deliver results. The main casualties of this? Your imagination and creativity.

The other casualties, which you might not expect, are honesty and good behaviour. I sometimes scratch my head at why people are surprised when ruthless performance and conformity cultures in sport, business, politics or the workplace result in poor behaviour. Because obeying rules isn't the same as buying-in. Even if you do what's expected, it will be temporary, fake and forced.

There are so many better ways to create inspiring workplaces and inspire people's will to be better. You can 'ensoul' uniforms, group identities and rituals without forcing uniformity.

Think of the Australian cricket team, who for more than 100 years have worn the baggy green cap at international Tests. 'There is no doubt that its aura provides Australian teams with a psychological edge,' says Mark Taylor, former captain. This is the same for any sports team who has done the work on understanding their history, identity and symbolism. Any badge, shirt, coat of arms or 'sacred' place can hold personal meaning.

You could see the way a person packs her kit bag – boots first, shin pads last – either as superstitious nonsense or as a helpful ritual. A bowler whispering his prayer to the ball before the start of play, the way someone laces their shoes or ties a ribbon can all create powerful individual and collective meaning without the need for control.

Being forced to stay in line will keep your fear levels running high. Not just day-to-day or year-to-year, but if you don't address it head on, for ever. All of us are tremendously inclined to repeat patterns until they are bust open and deliberately changed.

Is it time to make a stand?

Sports can be seen as the canary down the coalmine for the wider culture and society they are part of. Changes in sport culture don't stay in sport. They reflect what's happening in the rest of society, too.

Right now, there's a turning point in sport. You'll have seen evidence: the old-school, predatory, possessive, controlling, fear-generating ways are finally being challenged. Athletes and other professionals are speaking up to say that the way things used to be run is damaging. There's a new style of coaching and leadership coming in.

As sports journalist Vicki Hall wrote about Canadian ice hockey, 'the "what happens in the dressing room, stays in the dressing room" era is over'. She was describing the resignation of old-school-style head coach Bill Peters from the Calgary Flames in 2019, prompted by accusations of racism and physical abuse.

But if you're not in sport, what does that mean for you? Maybe you're getting through life just fine. Things are pretty good, you're not bombing out and everyone feels like a loser some days, right?

No. If you find yourself working or functioning in a fear environment, as described earlier in this chapter, the ideal scenario is that you raise your hand and say: 'This is not OK.'

But why *should* you have to speak up and take a stand against fear-provoking practices? Because it's important, if we want to win deep and live with less fear and more freedom. The more of us who challenge the status quo, the more change we will see.

This is not just me advising, 'Be brave'. Some people won't be able to speak up. You may not be in a position to make any kind of stand or challenge. If that's you, the next best thing is to get out. And if you can't do that, you can still use some of the ways to uncover and deal with fear that you'll read about later in the book.

However, if we do challenge fear-promoting cultures, we can transform the environments where people work and play. Then, at a personal and professional level, we'll see fear responses can be reduced for all of us.

If you are running a team or organisation, if you're a teacher or have a role of responsibility in a community or family, you can be the change too. Think about whether you perpetuate fear in any way that I've described, or even allow or ignore it. There's no blame here; the old ways of talking about success run deep. But please know that there is a better way you can lead, one where the result will be more fulfilment. And that's better for performance and results, too. Win–win.

This change is going to take some time. The old ways won't shift straight away. The idea that winning needs to be a serious business fuelled by fear is still a seductive and pervasive narrative to many. But nevertheless, very often change will come if we start to act.

CHAPTER 5

What happens to us in fear culture?

You've already heard about how fear is recycled via our beliefs, and so affects us in our workplaces and other environments. Now we're going to look at all the associated personal cost that living in a fear culture can bring. These effects are culture-wide, so I hope, as you read, you feel some of the burden of responsibility shift away from you. At the same time, I hope you start to recognise yourself in some of these examples.

Living in a fear culture doesn't have the same effect on everyone, as what happens will depend not only on your personality but on how you've been brought up and the beliefs and behaviours you've been exposed to. So what could living in a fear culture have done to you? It may have shrunk you, so you have stayed small in some ways, limiting your potential and what you can achieve. Fear can also stiffen you into rigid over-control of yourself and the people around you. And it can also push you into painful, burning shame. All of these things send you down a rabbit hole away from your real potential as a human being.

While what is about to follow may sound dark and gloomy, I hope it will give you insight into particular areas of your life to look at, clues to look out for. Because once you recognise that what you're experiencing is fear-based, you will be able to think about how best to use the ideas in the second part of the book, to help you overcome that fear.

Trapped by the 5 fear limits

What happens when you're surrounded by fear and scarcity? You shrink. (It would have been better to name psychologists like me 'anti-shrinks', because we want you to do the opposite!) You might recognise fear as limiting you in one – or likely more than one – of these five ways.

1. Fear spoils your fun

Are you the one who stays in the office late, answers emails in the evenings, insists on getting a head-start on work projects at the weekends? Then the fear track running in your background is that you have to sacrifice fun to win. And even when you do have time off, you don't relax.

If this is you, you'll have the sense that having a good time will get in the way of success. You may think prioritising fun is slacking off and you'll get caught out. Or it's a sign of low willpower and a lack of self-discipline.

Because fear is a fun thief in another way too. When you're a fear-driven person, everything feels like work. You might even cook dinner to impress or perform for someone, not for the sheer joy of putting ingredients together. Fun becomes only a distraction or a reprieve from the real purpose of life, which is avoiding not being good enough.

Is this *really* how you want to live? Can you think of a way that your life would be worse if you had a good time?

Fun, especially fun with people you trust, gives you a pop of feel-good chemicals and hormones. These include pleasurable endorphins, rewarding dopamine and maybe a side-order of loved-up oxytocin. By lowering tension and increasing positivity, fun enhances performance. And the relief it brings helps to stop you burning out from overwork, too.

Play comes naturally to us all. It switches us out of performance mode and makes us feel we can be free to be who we truly are. Making time for fun is about making space for soul. There are absolutely parts of pursuing your potential that may never be fun, like pre-season 'beep-tests' or revising for exams. But don't let fear close the door on the very best stuff of life.

2. Fear keeps you small

Fear might be the reason you keep yourself small and out of the way. You want to make sure you don't fail or get hurt.

If this is you, you're reluctant to speak up, settling instead for stagnant comfort. Fear makes you avoid what feels challenging. It wants you to get through the day and not have to delve into difficult emotions. You may unwittingly avoid great parts of yourself being seen, or exposed, in exchange for this easier life. Maybe you use being busy to avoid thinking about what else could be: you've got bills to pay, grades to get and goals to score, after all.

But perhaps it doesn't really feel all that easy after all, staying hidden or small?

Each of us draws the boundaries of what's realistic in our lives: how much we can earn, what work we can do, where we can live, the level of education we can reach. And although some of us have more practical limitations — for example, money, children, illness, elderly parents — most of us largely stay within our self-created limits.

Ask yourself: who drew those boundaries for me? Did I inherit an expectation to do a certain job, live in a particular place, have a set number of children? Is it fear that's making my boundaries too narrow?

You may have heard Marianne Williamson's famous passage from her book *A Return To Love*, as it was used by President Nelson Mandela in his inaugural speech in 1994. In it, she makes the point beautifully that we all have the ability to go beyond our fear-imposed boundaries:

> Our deepest fear is not that we are inadequate. Our
> deepest fear is that we are powerful beyond measure.
> It is our light, not our darkness that most frightens us.
> We ask ourselves, who am I to be brilliant, gorgeous,
> talented, fabulous? Actually, who are you not to be?

Personal growth is often presented as linear, about ticking off set goals. But it's more useful to imagine it as a journey. It's about broadening, deepening and expanding, rather than just improving. About growing *out* and not just up.

I call this wayfaring. As well as goals, this includes other kinds of development that come from making great memories, deep connections and vivid experiences. To be able to wayfare more, look at how much fear is stopping you exploring things you want to do, the things our cultures don't see as success. Wayfarers choose to get off the conventional path to success to expand, grow and have new experiences. For example, author and entrepreneur Dave Asprey had a successful career in Silicon Valley before he started a personal journey to improve his health, wrote five books on what he discovered about bio-hacking and founded the global health optimisation company Bulletproof.

Is fear limiting your beliefs about yourself? You might think, 'I'm not good with people, so I can't be management material'. Or, 'I am unlovable, so I can't ever have a lasting relationship'.

The growth mindset, an idea from professor of psychology at Stanford University Carol Dweck,[1] might help you shift limiting beliefs. Among other things Dweck showed that if schoolchildren believe they can get smarter, they try harder for longer, and so end up doing better than those who think intelligence is fixed.

> The passion for stretching yourself and sticking to
> it, even (or especially) when it's not going well, is
> the hallmark of growth mindset. This is the
> mindset that allows people to thrive during some of
> the most challenging times of their lives.

Try looking through the lens of the growth mindset at all the areas you'd like to improve, expand and change. If you believe you can become smarter, wiser, kinder, more compassionate, you up the chances. More specifically, if you believe you can learn French, become a people person, start running, get a degree, it's more likely to happen.

Sometimes growth can also mean letting go rather than gaining something. That might mean leaving a relationship or a job or choosing not to go for a promotion.

Making any change takes courage. Setting off to achieve anything is about risk and uncertainty and also fear. But it's worth doing: it's an extraordinary gift to be able to welcome growth in all directions.

3. Fear betrays your trust

When fear is dialled up, trust goes down. If you work or spend time in an environment like this, it can feel like people are out for themselves. Or that if you make a mistake, heads will roll. In some cases there may be a kind of loyalty based on conditional alliances; I'll scratch your back if you scratch mine. Living with any of the above will drain your energy.

Another way you can recognise a low-trust environment is the existence of in-groups who have their own knowledge and privileges. It's tough to be on the outside of these groups. But it's damaging to be on the inside too. Even if you are well liked and well accepted, when people who don't fit in are targeted or mocked, for example, being excluded from important information or even after-work drinks, trust gets paper-thin and fear gets a boost. It raises the spectre that, one day, the excluded person could be you.

This kind of trust isn't about whether someone is going to get the job done. It's about having belief in another person or people and their intentions. It comes from open-heartedness, inspires allegiance, love and faithfulness. And it's life-affirming.

You could see personal trust as an unfurling of tension and caution, something like a fern unfurling. The koru symbol, seen in Māori art, is based on the fern. Its spiral shape conveys the idea that even while it's opening outwards, there's a connection back to where it started. Similarly, when you open up and extend trust to another person, your own willingness to trust will also need to be renewed regularly.

Our goals are usually achieved alongside others. So apart from being draining, low trust limits you extending yourself and taking risks towards your goals.

4. Fear restricts your mental freedom

We all worry how other people see us. For some, this can be a crippling burden. Even genuinely confident people have those little spiky prods of anxiety about whether they looked like an idiot, or how they're being judged. The anxiety about how other people perceive you can eat into your mental freedom. At root, when you are thinking about someone else's opinion of you, you are feeling the fear that you're not good enough.

Mental freedom is the direct opposite of this fear. It's those rare and welcome moments when we are liberated from others' opinions. It's psychological spaciousness where you can apply yourself to whatever you want, or simply rest, without worry-traffic clogging up your mind.

You need mental freedom if you want to access both your gifts and their potential. Fear, by keeping us stuck in certain thoughts, stops us accessing our better intelligence or seeing opportunities. Fear, in effect, makes us more stupid.

But in modern life, all of our minds are busy, so busy. The key to mental freedom, then, is to gain control over your thoughts. You have to be mindfully aware both of what you are doing right now and how you are doing it. You have to keep working to balance letting go of unhelpful thoughts and acting. And you have to avoid getting caught in the Venus flytrap of your fearful mind and getting distracted.

If you do a martial art or meditate, you'll already know what mental freedom feels like, and other ways to get to this are explained more fully in chapter 7. As Bruce Lee said: 'Concentration is the root of all the higher abilities in man'. Martial artists use focus as a way of being fully conscious in the present moment, while staying sharply aware of what is happening within and around them.

Mental freedom works to fight fear because acceptance of the present moment and fear cannot coexist. Fear is about what might go wrong in the future, even if that future is only seconds away.

Just as blinking clears your vision, constantly returning your mind to the present clears it. But you have to actively choose to clear your mind, rather than succumb to the incessant river of chatter and nonsense. In fact, you'll always have to do this. But it's not a big deal, just a process of taking a deep exhale, checking where your attention is and bringing it back.

5. Fear shackles your expectations

A friend of mine, Aleta, uses a great expression I'll borrow to describe the limits people place on themselves or others; 'the tragedy of low expectations'. Low expectations says: people like me (or you) are not good enough so I won't expect much.

Expectations are the power behind your ambitions. Expectations set your course and help you believe, and help sprout the green shoots of your potential. When your expectations are limited, you may settle for less and stay under the ceiling that's set for you (or by you).

This can happen when specialness is overplayed. The idea takes hold that only certain types of exceptional beings can do something, and everyone else is likely to be underwhelming – you included. This fuels your fear of failure.

Across elite sport, I've spoken to a lot of very capable women who've told me how hard it is not to get pulled down by other's low expectations of what's possible in a male-dominated world. They know they're equal in intelligence, skill and character, but they also know that people often don't expect them to lead, raise their voices or take risks like their male counterparts. When their success is explained in terms of specialness (you're different), this pressures the woman to stay in line, not to make waves and risk their 'privileged' spot.

Another way expectations are edited is when categories of people are seen as more than, or less than others because of the biases we have and unconscious judgements we make. Sometimes these are on the basis of skin colour, ethnicity, nationality, gender identity or socio-economic background. These are all qualities that have nothing to do with talent and the ability to be a winner.

This happens in particular for people with disabilities. I watched in awe in 2019 as Lee Spencer, a former Royal Marine and amputee from Devon in England, completed the 3800-mile solo transatlantic row from mainland Europe to South America in 60 days. His time smashed the able-bodied record by an incredible 36 days. His nights and days were spent facing 40–50-foot waves, surviving deep isolation and physical pain, while only taking two hours' sleep at a time.

Of course he could have failed. In fact, it was likely. But nothing, especially fear, was telling Lee Spencer that his disability meant he should lower his expectations. This is what he told me:

> When the row started to take shape as an idea, I quickly realised there was an able-bodied record of 96 days. I thought, if I beat that, I'm not defined by disability. While I was rowing, I had a real eureka moment. I realised I was still the same person I always was. That I was wrong to try and define who I was as if it was someone totally new because I had a disability. That got me thinking about how we in society define disabled people in such a limited way.

This quote from playwright and actor Neil Marcus, a key player in the development of disability culture, speaks volumes about the kind of fear-less mindset and imagination that creates enduring winners like Lee:

> Disability is not a brave struggle or 'courage in the face of adversity'. Disability is an art. It is an ingenious way to live.

When no one expects anything much of us, we quit more quickly and limit our possibilities under the heading 'not for my kind'. It's worth remembering that our narratives are self-fulfilling. Don't wait for someone else to rewrite yours. The people who are holding the mic don't always want to share it.

I feel particularly saddened when I hear people crumple up their dreams and put them in their back pocket because they don't think 'the kind of person they are' can be a winner. Low expectations are different from low self-esteem. Low self-esteem says, 'I'm not good enough', while low expectations say, 'People like me are not good enough'. Examples might be:

'I'm not going to raise my hand even though I know the answer because I'm one of the dumb kids.'

'I'm not going to put myself forward for the leadership because it's always the white guys that get that role.'

'I would just be happy to pass. My family aren't really academic.'

'I'm not the sort of person who gets that sort of job.'

'Women are never going to be accepted in that kind of environment.'

Not many people who feel like winners in life got to the peak and found themselves completely surprised. Grateful, maybe, but not surprised. You have to work, commit, endeavour and most of all get over your own fear to set great expectations for yourself. Especially if you are surrounded by people who set tragically low ones for you.

In his book *Natives: Race and Class in the Ruins of Empire*, musician, political activist, journalist, poet and author Akala gives a sharp account of the low expectations set for him as a mixed-race schoolboy growing up in north London in the 1980s.[2] He paints a picture of how teachers' biases and fears smothered the educational expectations of non-white children, dragging many down into apathy, regardless of their potential.

Akala himself was put in a special needs group, despite his clear intelligence. He was repeatedly told to talk less – or not at all – in the classroom. He tells a story of a friend who had a similar experience at school: 'The teacher went on to tell his mother that her son was too smart, he knew all the answers and that he was "not giving the white kids a chance". If she could just get him to be quiet, that would be wonderful.'

Expectations aren't about variations in talent. After all, different activities require different capabilities. They are about keeping hold of your possibilities even while admiring incredible others. Try not to put a limit on what you think you are capable of. And don't shut down, stay small or chase less because you're not sure that you should be in the arena. Excellence can be found anywhere.

We suffer with shame

While fear limits are a relatively direct effect of living in a fear culture, shame runs deeper. Everyone feels shame, but not everyone is incapacitated by it. You have to be primed for it, have had early experiences that tell you that you are unworthy, bad or wrong in the core of your very being. That doesn't mean shame is unusual, because that early experience doesn't have to be an extreme one: it can be as commonplace as regularly being publicly told off or shown up.

If that has happened to you, you'll always be ready to experience shame, the acute rush of humiliation and distress that comes from feeling like you are not enough. Then, if you're surrounded by fear, it's only a small step to replace the plain old disappointment of failing with a much more damaging flare-up of shame.

Shame has a particular facial expression and demeanour. Take the Australian cricketers revealed to be involved in the ball-tampering scandal in 2018: in interviews their eyes are cast downward, their gestures submissive. In fact, they look deeply in pain — because they are. And even though your shame is unlikely to be shown on television, it's still incredibly painful.

Steve Smith, the Australian team captain, cried as he confessed and apologised. Even though the cricketers had done the wrong thing, there's something cold and inhuman behind enforcing a televised apology. It's the modern equivalent of the humiliation of being put in the stocks.

A similar thing happened when, in 2012, the Australian swimmers returned from the London Olympics with a medal haul that was way below what was expected. After details of some of the team's bad behaviour emerged — such as misusing prescription drugs, breaking curfew to knock on each other's doors at night, drinking alcohol and energy drink concoctions in camp close to events — some of the swimmers involved were forced to confess their misdemeanours on television.

I was asked to write a culture review on the team just after they returned. My conclusion was that although the athletes were out of order, the deeper issues lay with long-term problems in the organisation, leadership and the toxic culture. And yet, the public — or at least the tabloid press — demanded a public, televised show of humiliation.

Why do we think shaming someone will change their behaviour or is the best way to rectify the situation? Because it does neither.

There are less lazy methods of helping people to change their behaviour, such as connection and care. Indeed, that was the kind of positive guidance that was missing from the Australian swim team and has been addressed since.

As Brené Brown taught us in her TED Talk 'Listening to Shame',[3] shame isn't the same as guilt. In her words, guilt is 'sorry I made a mistake' while shame is 'sorry, I am a mistake'.

Guilt is useful because it keeps us aligned with our best selves. It's when you feel bad for doing something that you shouldn't have, or not doing something that you should have. And it's often associated with morals and principles, with 'shoulds' and wanting to be better.

These are some times you might feel guilt: you didn't pull your weight on a project that failed. You bumped a car and left without putting a note on the windscreen. You cheated on your partner. Guilt can be a strong emotion, but if you can make up or apologise for what you did or didn't do, it allows you to make amends and do better.

Shame, on the other hand, can make you feel completely worthless to your core and erode your self-esteem. You can see why we hate to feel it. And to feel it, you don't have to have done anything at all.

In fact, shame is often a response to someone else's action. That could be being called a 'slut' at the school bus stop or being abused by racists. Or being told that you are too fat, too dumb, too poor. Being divorced, sacked, dropped or mocked. Shame makes you feel discredited, disrespected and injured. And that injury happens at a soul level.

Both the swimmers and the cricketers did the wrong thing; they knew that and so did we. Guilt and an apology would be appropriate here. But because of their humiliating television appearances, and all the negative attention they received, their guilt risked turning inwards, into shame.

Most of the time, shame and anxiety go hand in hand. If you anticipate a situation where you might feel shame – one where there's a possibility of rejection, such as a date, presenting an idea at work, meeting a new partner's family – this can pre-fuel your fear of not being good enough, so you want to get away or hide. Before athletes perform, they can already be thinking about the embarrassment and shame they'll feel if don't succeed.

An organisation that uses guilt to motivate might tell you that you didn't make the grade because you didn't put in the work and this is what you need to do about it. One that uses shame will tell you that you didn't make the grade because you are not good enough. And it may compound the shame by doing this in public.

Consider the following two examples, shared with me by female elite athletes. In both cases, the team coaches want their athletes to reduce their Body Mass Index (BMI), a measure of their fat vs muscle make-up and an indicator of optimal fitness.

The coach of team A sets a four-week intensified training and nutritional programme. She lets the players know that at the end of four weeks, she will be expecting them to wear a new skin-tight Lycra uniform – which will clearly show the results – for training as well as games.

The coach gathers the whole group to share the markers she expects them to achieve to give them a professional advantage. These markers are within a range and the coach explains this is because she expects variation depending on body type and roles. She also expects everyone to reach their own personal best. The coach outlines the support the athletes can have, and heartily encourages them to give it their best effort for the team. Finally, she shares how hard she found this aspect of her own pro-career and what a difference it made to her fitness when she finally cracked it. The players are encouraged to buddy up.

The players are nervous; they don't want to fail publicly. But they take it on with humour. They share tips on their group WhatsApp about how 'a good wax and a suntan can take off ½ inch'. One leaves a motivational message tied to a carrot stick in another's locker. They start a weekly Lindt chocolate Lindor Ball challenge that's awarded to the biggest loser to huge applause and with a tongue-in-cheek acceptance speech. The coach and physical preparation staff are invited too.

In Team B, the coach gathers the group for a presentation of what good BMI looks like in athletes from opposition teams. He talks about how much respect he has for these other athletes and that they have achieved their results through strong character and true professionalism.

During the session, the coach brings out a six-foot-high laminated chart with every athlete on the team ranked in order of BMI. He sticks it to the wall in the team room. The label at the top of the chart reads 'fattest player' and the label at the bottom of the chart reads 'best player'. The coach asks the five players with the highest BMI to explain why they are so far off-target and what they are going to do about it before the next tournament. The players blush and are clearly uncomfortable, but they mumble through their answers, which he takes as a sign of them being sufficiently embarrassed – shamed – to change.

The coach also asks the captain to let the group know that anyone who doesn't meet the target will risk being dropped. There is no follow-up and no information about when the topic will be revisited. The players – unsurprisingly – are anxious. While some manage to lower their BMI in the following weeks, some also report feeling on tenterhooks and wanting to avoid the coach. Several start or scale up existing damaging weight-management practices.

Can you see how in Team B the coach used shame and the threat of shame to manipulate? Even if he had got every single player to lower her BMI, it would have been achieved through the players being desperate to avoid rejection. In Team A, the coach worked on deepening the identity of the team as professionals, building on their belief in each other; Team B's coach used comparison, and had no clear time frame. Crucially, he added a much bigger threat: that they would be dropped.

As you can see from Team B's response, shaming isn't a good teacher or motivator. It's too painful. When your greatest need is to avoid shame, you're not worried about right and wrong, you're worried about self-protection.

Shame dehumanises us, and to get real change and lasting results, we need to rehumanise. I'm not suggesting we should lower standards, and that athletes – or anyone – who breaks the rules shouldn't face the consequences. But when someone makes a mistake, we shouldn't keep feeding on their pain. Shaming damages the person it happens to, and it damages all of us, as we all end up fearful that it could happen to us, too.

We become over-controlling

In a culture that's fuelled by fear, another common way to deal with pressure is over-control. We do this because we never want to be caught out, to be criticised or, even worse, have to experience the corrosive emotion of shame.

Our attempt to take control can take lots of different forms. We may become overly controlling of ourselves, make sure we are perfect, or judge ourselves harshly against rigid standards. Or we may become inflexible with other people and so judge or manipulate them too.

There is a positive side to control, of course. Control brings order, order brings focus, focus brings a sense of calm. It can feel quite soothing, as any of us who love a list will attest to. And you need structures and systems to get things done effectively and efficiently.

Ideally, control offers a counterweight to your impulses, moods and distractibility. It allows you to be productive, keeps your ambitions and efforts focused. It is closely linked with discipline, another tool that ensures you stick to the right codes, rules and routines for the best outcomes. Both of these are excellent mechanisms to use, but not to be used *by*.

However, when your head is full of *not-good-enough* fear, your way of compensating might be to work so damn hard that you cannot fail. Control tightens up and discipline becomes your religion.

Other people might say to you, 'Shouldn't you take a break?' or 'Why don't you take a day off?' And you might think, 'Are you kidding?' If you are in control mode, true rest is a luxury. Distraction, entertainment and numbing yourself with TV, alcohol or whatever does it for you will give you some respite . . . but rest? That would be ridiculous.

You might turn these inflexible high standards outwards towards other people, too: becoming the boss who never lets up and emails her team every evening, the parent who pushes his child too hard, the friend who judges others for not keeping up to their own high standards of grooming or housekeeping or fitness.

How can you tell the difference between passionate productivity and fear-generated discipline? When it's the good kind, you feel involved, stable and invested. You're full of creativity, ideas and imagination. But the controlling kind? For me, that particular energy is like a nettle-sting rash after 15 minutes; irritating enough to keep you uncomfortable, but tolerable enough to bear. It's physical impatience: your foot won't stop tapping under the table and you're grinding your teeth in traffic.

I've lived this feeling. In my early to mid-thirties (I'm now 49), I decided to take up distance running. This can offer you fantastic mental and physical challenges. For me, though, running quickly combined my anxious over-productivity and my controlling need to prove myself.

Because I was fear-fuelled, I never really gave running the space it needed. I wedged it around an already full life, working and studying, stealing the time from my relationships. The blend of rigidly planned training sets and goals I could will myself through was intoxicating. It was perfect: I could really do a number on myself.

Completing my first marathon felt pretty good. My ego was stoked and I was so thrilled and grateful that other people's praise landed on me solidly. But because productivity was my religion, I did a second, then a 45km race and a few 100km walking/running events.

I told myself they were fun and kept me fit, but in fact they were punishing grounds where I could totally ignore my body telling me I had gone too far. I was running on adrenalin, gaunt in body and spirit because my over-control was being fuelled by a fear of not being good enough so it could never be satisfied.

Seventy-two kilometres into one 100km race, I ran out of fuel: I was dehydrated and in pain after picking up a hip injury at around the 60km mark. It was 2 a.m., freezing cold and pitch-black in rural Australia. This was a four-person event, and as my body gave up, my mind was raging with anger and shame that I was going to fail but my teammates were going to succeed and be better than me.

Once I had some electrolytes and saline back in my body, I had a shocking realisation: my fear-fuelled need to prove myself had landed me with a super-sized resentment of my dear teammates, people I loved. The blisters on my feet were nothing in comparison to the blistering realisation of my fear of not being good enough.

When we overuse control and discipline, as I did, they tighten into concrete ways of being that offer little flex and room for imagination. This is a good question to ask yourself: what is fear's role in my need for control? How is fear directing my energy?

A few years after that Australian race, I did a solo back-to-back trek up Mount Kenya and Mount Kilimanjaro, in total a 10,000km climb. The lessons from that cold night in Australia had lodged deep in me. I trained and planned and prepared as well as for any previous endurance event, but this time was utterly different.

For a start, I decided I would really experience the world around me: those mountains with their jagged edges and sweeping terraces, their valleys of cactus and forests of rhododendron. I wanted to hear them, take them in. I still wanted to get to the top of both, but this time I had an appetite for the journey. I also wanted to spend time with the people who were alongside me: my hired guide, Kingston, his brother Chieftain, the cook, and my tentmates on Kilimanjaro.

Ascending to the top of Mount Kenya in a blizzard, my legs and back burned, my eyes were stinging almost shut and my knees wanted to give way. But this time I was filled with laughter and joy, spirit and openness. I have a picture at the summit, which still makes my heart sing, of wonderful Kingston and me both in a Warrior III yoga pose in swirling snow.

The final route to the summit of Kilimanjaro was teeming with people. Some I saw had something to prove to their egos; smiles stretched into grimaces with fear of inadequacy at each obstacle they met, urgency frosted on to them at -15 degrees for the pre-dawn push. But others were working together, strangers and friends pulling each other up the mountain, helping each other put their frozen gloves back on rather than worrying about their selfies at the summit sign.

The exchange of smiles and warm words seemed to melt away doubt and give people that extra boost. With less than 500 metres to the top, I saw a woman give up her own summit to walk back down with her buddy who, having thrown up one too many times, needed to go to a lower altitude.

You could say that everyone who made the summit executed their plan perfectly well. But it's the tone of their winning that made the difference.

What had changed for me? After all, the humanity and generosity was on offer in the 100km races and marathons too. But I had been so lost inside my own fearful mind that I could not see or feel the vibrant energy between people. And it is that energy that gets each of us over the line in life way more often than our rigid plans.

Mental well-being

'Fear is the path to the dark side'

– Yoda, *The Phantom Menace*

Mental well-being is not a given, so I'm thrilled that talking about it is starting to lose its stigma. But we still treat it as an individual phenomenon, something that happens within each person. We need to think about it in terms of the person and their cultures, their environments.

A notable exception is the work of Amy Edmondson, a professor at Harvard Business School and author of *The Fearless Organization*. She shared with us all the concept of psychological safety in the workplace that shows that when people feel safe to take risks and be vulnerable at work, this leads to their best performance. I see this as an idea that can expand to truly change the way we operate in all of life's settings.

The problem is that if you see mental well-being as an individual issue, the solutions can also only be personal, i.e., supporting that person to get help and to get well. Of course this is critical but what about the fact we live in environments that recycle fear and anxiety, and chronically grind down our mental well-being, individually and collectively?

Think of emotional well-being as a continuum. Each of us will fluctuate along it, both up and down. There are many reasons for this, but two that I'd like to explore here are your environments, and the quality and character of your relationships.

If you are stuck in environments and ways of being in which fear is deliberately used as a tool to make you comply and perform, the cost to your mental well-being can simply be too high. You don't need to add more fear, tolerate more fear, be the most feared, to be perfect or even conquer everyone else. All of these things are mentally exhausting. They suck you away from your true best and wear away at your well-being.

That said, I am endlessly awed by the resilience people show. And by the vulnerable and brave way some people respond to adversity. Because you can cope in one of two ways:

There is invulnerability. This involves shutting down, ignoring, avoiding and internalising your fears. It results in you feeling like a fraud in your own life because you're keeping up a pretence, even when you're coming apart at the seams. It also means you have to cope alone, which leads to disconnection, not only from others but from yourself.

There is a second way: being resilient. This might include being free to be yourself, to express your vulnerability honestly. And being able to express and therefore take some power out of your fears and anxieties. A final part of this is to be able to work out and work through your pain.

An inspiring example of this is actor and activist Jameela Jamil, who has been publicly vulnerable about who she is and what she believes in. She has shared details about her mental health, specifically that she tried to take her own life, due to having post-traumatic stress disorder. Her tweet went on to say: 'Ask for help if you need it. Because things can turn around. I promise.'

She's also been open about her struggle with her body image, starting the I Weigh body positivity movement to empower others too. And, more recently, she came out as queer, writing 'I didn't come from a family with *anyone* openly out. It's also scary as an actor to openly admit your sexuality, especially when you're a brown female in your thirties.'

The more completely you can be yourself, the more fully and consciously you can be in the world without hiding. Even your weird, twisted and awkward vulnerabilities (we all have them!) are better lived than locked up inside you.

I have been on the sidelines many times when someone in public life mucks something up and needs to face it publicly. Where a fear culture is strong, they generally feel the need to pretend – and so suffer much more than necessary.

Yet it isn't surprising that people don't always want to share their real feelings. The acceptable response to failure in modern Western culture is to be contrite, apologetic and stoic, whatever you're actually feeling. That was the television performance expected of and given by the Australian Olympic swimming team, and of the Australian cricketers involved in the ball-tampering scandal, too.

You are supposed to be ready to disinfect the failure and move on. Scripting your emotions and pretending is considered preferable to being honest about how you feel, and risking being torn down. After a short 'self-indulgent' moment, vulnerability, pain and anxiety are no longer allowed, in favour of upbeat courage, positivity and humility.

But whitewashing a person's naturally diverse emotions, cleaning up too quickly, can cause mental strain. And life is not all about being happy, content and unrelentingly positive.

How can you know what to face down if you hide it behind a facade of positivity? How can you live, work, perform with soul if you can only show your glossy side? How can anyone help you if you have it all locked down away from view?

From a psychological point of view, whatever's in us that's exiled and hidden can grow hostile and ultimately dangerous. If you squash anger down so no one can see it, you can't honour that anger, face it and deal with it. Fear operates in the same way.

From the outside in

Recognising that it's not all you, knowing you have to deal with it from the outside, means you are more able to recognise fear in its many forms. Then you'll know when it's more likely to arise and so run interference on it. If you don't realise what is happening, you're not even going to notice when you need to intervene.

This is true whatever form your fear twists into, whether it's becoming over-controlling because your boss is so critical, or you've felt shame in a similar situation or group of people in the past, or you can see how you're self-sabotaging by limiting or editing yourself in some way. Later in the book, from part three onwards, is all about how to do this.

The next section explains how human beings are perfectly designed to respond to fear, how we're always biologically primed to go into a fear reaction. (So in effect, it's a double whammy because you've got fear coming from the inside, too.) Then, we'll look at ways to boss this kind of raw biological fear and start to develop a truly fear less mindset.

PART 2

Be prepared to be scared

CHAPTER 6

How (and why) our brains create fear

You drive too fast into a bend and feel the wheels start to skid.

You pick up the phone to hear: 'I'm afraid I have some bad news.'

You are running late at night and, in your peripheral vision, you see the bushes rustle.

Fear feels like the jolt of a thousand volts of electricity shooting up your chest. The fear response is a self-protective mechanism designed to help keep us alive. This chapter explains why it's natural and hard-wired into us, and how it mobilises our brain and body to react to a dangerous or life-threatening situation.

The problem is, when you're in any one of the different fear-provoking environments I've been describing, you're always ready to react, even though the situation isn't likely to be life-threatening.

This raw, animal fear is simply a message saying: Danger! Get ready to respond! So only the tiniest of split seconds after you sense the bush rustling, you've jumped out of the way.

Next, your 'thinking brain' kicks in to analyse the situation. Depending on whether that rustle was a mouse or a mugger, you might have a blip of anxiety and a quick rush of adrenalin through your legs, or a wave of sheer panic. *In-the-moment* fear takes you over. Your only focus is on avoiding or dealing with the source of the fear.

The issue is that our fear response is extremely active, always ready. So not only are you living in a fear-filled environment, but you're always primed to go into fear.

What you *can* do is learn to quieten the fear response quickly when it arises and when it isn't helpful for you. This is something we will talk about in chapter 7. Before learning the specific techniques, it's useful to look at how it affects your body and brain. If you can name and recognise the fear feelings, mental and physical, and understand that the process is not only normal but expected, you will begin to feel more in control.

Why you're primed for fear

Your incredible, extremely complex brain has what you could call an evolutionary design flaw. It processes negative emotions – especially fear – super-fast, and other types of information more slowly. So your brain readily defaults to distress and suffering, and it is particularly good at jumping into fear.

While our human ancestors have been around for a couple of million years, evolutionary biologists suggest that it was only around 100,000 years ago that the modern human being evolved. And it was only roughly 50,000 years ago that a part of the brain mutated and evolved to give us the conscious capacity to reason, plan, be creative, use imagination, feel empathy, develop morality and use language. This 'new circuitry' allows you to think about and decide how you want to live. In fact, it's the part that's decided to read this book.

Your 'old brain circuitry' – the part you share with ancient man, other mammals and reptiles – has stayed exactly the same. You didn't get a full upgrade during our human evolution; the old is still operating alongside the new. And there is a constant battle raging between the two about how you should respond to your environment.

The old circuitry, which includes the amygdala fear-centre, is all about survival. It is a neural network that has stood the test of a million years of natural selection. Almost everything that happens in this part of your brain – instincts, unconscious emotional and behavioural impulses, and primitive survival anxieties – is unconscious or unknown to you and has been laid down over eons of evolution as well as more recent generations in body memories and experiences. Scientists now think that your unconscious brain makes up a very large part of your responses to the world around you. In fact, you're much more instinctively driven that you might like to think.

Your ability to work out if something is desirable and good or dangerous and bad was fully formed before you were even born. You were able to process fear before just about any other brain function – fear is a pretty big deal for you and for all of us.

Your unconscious is also formed by what happened in your early life, especially before you had language and reason and could understand concepts. In fact, these abilities aren't fully developed for the first couple of decades of life, and so especially as a baby and infant when you were most dependent and vulnerable, your brain development and world view were shaped dramatically by your parents and caregivers' communication style and their responsiveness to your needs. You worked out if you were safe, protected and cared for – or not – from their non-verbal communications and behaviour. And you sent this information straight to your unconscious, where it still is today.

In contrast, the new networks that came to regulate the amygdala, that allow you to act from reason and choice among other things, didn't finish developing until you were in your early to mid-twenties. All your early life, your highly adaptable, highly plastic and mouldable brain couldn't do much at all about the amount of fear you felt, whether you could manage your emotions, and how much self-worth you felt. That's why teenagers can appear bold and reckless: they don't have fully developed 'brain brakes'.

Even now, your amygdala is all about survival, trying to keep you alive and find you a genetically superior mate. It doesn't see any difference between your world today and the world when your ancient relatives were genuinely under mortal threat from predators and rivals. So whether you're in an inconvenient traffic jam with people honking at you or you're being held up at knife-point, it responds as if things were going downhill fast for you and you might not make it out alive. It's not very discerning.

In the meantime, your newer circuitry is trying to work out the fine details of competing projects, develop your character, moderate social behaviour and understand the meaning of life. This is the part that can find a cure for cancer, create breathtaking art and music, and build artificial intelligence, to name a few things.

So you can see the tension. One system in your brain is completely focused on preservation, and has evolved to avoid risks and stay vigilant. The other is dealing with expansion, innovation and using creativity to build on ideas.

The two systems work together in an uneasy coalition. So very often on any given day – or, more accurately, at any given second – there's a big, unseen fight over who's in charge. This constant pull in opposite directions causes you distress, even though you're not likely to know why you are feeling it.

For example, say your partner is going on a work trip for three days. You feel overwhelmingly anxious despite the fact you trust them 100 percent and you know where they're going is safe. So you can't understand the way you feel.

Or it could be that you are generally confident, but in a particular situation around particular people you become irrationally defensive and uncomfortable.

In both cases, an old fear from your deep unconscious is rattling you. In an attempt to make sense of things, it's easy to misattribute your feelings to something that's not the real cause. You might look for evidence that your partner is going to stray or worry about their method of transport, for example, but your unconcious fear is of being abandoned.

The two systems don't just have opposing goals, they also have different languages and, crucially, they operate at different speeds. Your old circuitry has a sneaky advantage because it works super-fast. You don't have to stop and think (in fact, you cannot 'think' or reason) from this system.

This is how it works. Going back to that rustle in the bushes while you're running. Before you can even think 'what the hell is that?', you have jumped out of the way. You have reacted from what's called somatic or body memory, part of the workings of your unconscious mind. Immediately the amygdala is triggered by the rustle in the bushes, it sends a signal to your nervous system to get ready to fight or flee.

Half a second later, your thoughts kick in. It takes this long because having a thought is way more complex and takes a little longer. Your cerebral cortex scans for meaning through your various forms of knowledge and understanding – your memory banks, your body, your past experiences and emotions – like Siri browsing Google, except quicker.

You may feel as if you're living in the present and you probably feel as if, most of the time, your conscious mind is running the show. But the upshot of these two brain circuitries and their varying speeds means that your conscious thoughts are a step behind the amygdala brain and its connections to your vast and mysterious unconscious mind. You don't notice the gap, of course, but your reality isn't quite your reality. Hard to get your head around, I know.

That's why only using logic – for example, telling yourself there's no reason to be scared – won't necessarily turn off your fear. Fear comes from a deeper place than your logical mind, from your unconscious. It may not even be showing up as raw fear: it may come up as all kinds of anxieties and negative emotions.

The fear response: physical

So, what happens when you sense that rustle in the bushes? When a fear response is triggered, it begins a massive cascade of chemicals and reactions all over your body and brain. This is red alert, physically and neurologically.

First, it interrupts the usually stable message between your body and brain that says things are Situation Normal. Your central nervous system sends a message to your heart via the vagus nerve to tell it to get ready for action.

Your body is flooded with adrenalin, your danger-opportunity hormone. Your heart starts pumping harder, which can leave you short of breath, even hyperventilating (if the stimulus lasts long enough). It diverts blood towards the major muscle groups that you'd need to use to run or to face a challenge and away from those organs and extremities where it's needed less. This is why you feel tension in your thighs, shoulders, neck and back, and sometimes cold hands or feet. But at the same time, your palms are beginning to sweat because your body is already preparing not to overheat during whatever emergency action you go for, fight or flight.

Your legs and hands might start to tremble, and you might feel dizzy because of a shift in the oxygen–carbon-dioxide exchange in your body. But even if you feel like fainting, it's pretty unlikely because your blood pressure is spiking.

You may feel nauseous or have butterflies as your heart diverts blood away from the digestive system. It also diverts it away from your bladder. That explains why, in the changing rooms before a big game, you'll see athletes going to the bathroom so many times.

Your mouth gets dry because your brain–body messaging says that this is no time to stop and eat. Your liver starts to convert glycogen into glucose to fuel your muscles, instead of any other work it was doing.

Your vision changes. Your pupils dilate to let in more light to allow you to see your challenge or challenger better. You might experience narrowed or tunnel vision, where your focus is sharp and singular but you lose some of your peripheral vision.

To help you prepare for bad outcomes, your mind repeatedly scans your negative memories for information about what might happen next.

The fear response: mental and emotional

Fear affects feelings, thoughts and behaviours in quite dramatic ways.

Crucially, the fear response shapes your ability to process information. Cognitive processing slows, particularly anything like complex decision-making or critical thinking. Studies estimate that a person's IQ can drop up to 15 points when under threat.[4]

The sad truth is, we all become a little more stupid when we are overtaken by fear.

You lose perspective because your focus narrows dramatically to just two areas: what you know and what your negative memories tell you. Fear makes you more defensive and less open. You make short-term choices and shut down risks of all kinds. You go for what you already know, killing creativity.

You're more likely to get tribal when scared, shutting down any diverse thinking or unfamiliar voices. But at the same time, you stop behaving in a social way, retreat into yourself to get on with the business of surviving. This is down to the result of neuroception, how your nervous system judges whether you're safe or not. When scared, you're more likely to perceive others as a threat. You lose some of your ability to judge people's facial expressions too, making misunderstandings more likely.

So you can see, if your life is fuelled by fear, how it can have a damaging effect on your ability to function but, even more, to be fulfilled and happy.

Combining all of the above, the physical, mental and emotional, there are four fear responses: you either prepare to fight, take flight, you freeze or you appease. You may be more inclined towards one or more of these; we all have our personal patterns.

Fight – You advance. You prepare to tackle the challenge head on, move towards it vigorously, get angry and feel physically emboldened. You might raise your voice or square up physically.

Flight – You retreat. You look to escape as quickly as possible and you're physically ready to run like the wind.

Freeze – You feel stuck, numb, you play dead, go quiet, go missing, hide, tune out or check out from the situation in some way.

Appease – You show submission in your body posture by cringing, dropping your head, lowering your eyes, looking away, or you use your words in immediate efforts to soothe the other person or calm the situation.

Each time it's activated, the fear response takes around 15 to 20 minutes to reset biologically. If the source of fear continues, then your adrenals continually produce the stress hormone cortisol as you stay on high alert. If this happens often enough and for long enough, your adrenals become fatigued and your immune system tanks.

Eventually, you end up ready to react at even a slight provocation. You lose your ability to slow down and properly evaluate before you enter this reactive state. Long-term fear can affect your metabolism, memory, inflammation, blood pressure and blood sugar levels. It can also contribute to psychological disturbances such as depression, anxiety, loss of satisfaction and burnout.

When fear goes deeper

It's easy to recognise *in-the-moment* fear, the kind that naturally shows up in high-intensity moments, then passes by. Examples of *in-the-moment* fear might be as simple as the fear of missing a shot or messing up a speech. But fear isn't always clean and obvious like this.

In the introduction, I wrote briefly about this kind of *not-good-enough* fear, the kind that's less easy to identify. This is when your mind distorts fear into stress about the past or the future — we often call this anxiety. This is fear of what might happen or what did happen, and what that means for our survival, whether this is a real threat or not.

When fear shape-shifts into these more chronic and vampiristic anxiety-based forms of negativity, it can show up in lots of different ways that don't, at first glance, look anything like raw fear.

Fear could be behind the fact that there are things you don't want to do or say. Or you'd rather give up than try and fail. Or you're not being true to yourself.

It could be affecting your relationships, or make you overly clingy or want to stay disconnected from people around you. Fear can make you hide parts of yourself from other people. And it can distort into perfectionism, jealousy, being angry, bitchy or being judgemental.

But how can any of these agitated-based behaviours really be about fear?

If you think of fear as the root emotion, then from it comes a whole variety of these anxiety-based emotions and behaviours that sour your life and sap your energy. Here are some of the most common ways that fear can distort:

- When you feel jealousy, at root you'll find a fear of not being lovable.
- When you get sucked into perfectionism, at root you'll find a fear of failing.
- When you want to judge people or you feel judged, at root you'll find a fear of inadequacy.
- When you feel you have to keep yourself separate, at root you'll find your fear of being rejected.

As I've already explained, at the bottom of that pile of twisted roots is one big, overwhelming and ultimately human fear: the fear of not being enough, and therefore being abandoned. Because as a human being, this is what we all fear more than anything else.

It's these fears about not being good enough that cause much of your suffering and get in the way of your fulfilment. These murky fears are the real terrorists in your life. So the largest part of this book – sections three to four – is going to give you ideas about how to tackle them.

Take charge of fear

Fear of both kinds may arrive regularly. And whether it's *in-the-moment* fear or *not-good-enough* fear, it will rarely go away on its own.

The truth is, most of the time, you can't control the fear stimulus. You are still facing down that 50-foot wave, about to take your driving test, or getting ready to stand up and make a speech at your best friend's wedding. And you may also still feel at the whim of your self-critic popping up every five minutes, or your fear of being vulnerable. No amount of hoping is going to shift it.

The answer is that you need to deliberately change your response to any kind of fear. You can shift this by changing your behaviour, your physical focus, your mental attention and, importantly, the stories you tell yourself about it.

This deliberate change is part of what we can do as human beings: adapt to our environment. In a long-term evolutionary sense, all creatures either adapt to the pressures around them or, eventually, they don't survive. What's different for human beings is that we can actively participate in changing. We don't need to passively wait for change, we can decide to be different, better, smarter.

The good news? That means you are not helpless and passive against most of your everyday inner turmoils. And nor do you have to be a victim of the fear-promoting environments you find yourself in, or the fear-provoking relationships you have in your life.

You have the incredible advantage of being able to retrain and rewire your brain by doing things differently. You can do this by choosing, acting and focusing differently. You decide how to adapt, on purpose, rather than let circumstances happen to you.

For *in-the-moment* fears, the ones that show up at critical moments, that means preparing techniques that will help keep you calm and composed. That's what chapter 7 is about: all the techniques to tackle fears as they come up.

When it comes to *not-good-enough* fears, you're going to have to go deeper, which is the subject of chapter 8 onwards. You can't squash them down, because they will spring back up. And you can't prune them with positive thinking or fix them with tricks.

If you want to stop them taking over, you have to first take an honest look at what you are fearful of and how it is show-ing up in your life before you try to solve it. You have to become aware of what is provoking your fear in your envir-onment, then have a good look at what is happening inside you. You have to pull the fear out by the roots and examine what you're dealing with: you need to see, face and replace your fear.

And if you deal with your *not-good-enough* fears, you'll find you can handle your *in-the-moment* fears better too. Because if you knew you would never be loved less, never be abandoned or rejected or judged, wouldn't you be able to han-dle so much more pressure? You'd be able to, for example, get up and talk in front of people without anxiety (assuming you've done the technique work).

A less fearful life isn't going to arrive in the post. But you can evolve yourself, with the see-it-face it-replace-it approach. Like any other part of yourself that you want to change, you have to put some effort in and commit to working on the change. But you have the brain power to reflect, consider, imagine and relate with more love, less fear.

Do this, and you'll get a high return on your investment: more ease, less suffering and a mindset of abundance.

CHAPTER 7
Bossing *in-the-moment* fear

When fear drops in uninvited at a critical moment, it may feel impossible to deal with. It's natural, when you feel the adrenalin begin to course through you, to think you are about to snap or lose the plot. You might start checking out the emergency exits, ready to run. Or feel your heart beating so hard in your chest that you think you're going to die of the panic.

In this chapter, I will lay out a whole range of different techniques you can use to prepare yourself for *in-the-moment* fear, and help you deal with it when it arises. Remember: fear is simply a warning signal, a feeling or energy that you do not have to give attention to, especially if there is no real mortal danger. And you can boss it, whether it's expected or takes you by surprise. By the end of this chapter, you'll have a whole range of fear-bossing techniques to choose from.

What to do with your fear

Fear will come to flip you over. It's inevitable. It's your next move – your thoughts and response – that will make all the difference.

One of the people I admire most in his willingness to face into this kind of *in-the-moment* fear is Lee Spencer, the ex-Marine you've already read about, who rowed the 3,800 miles of the Atlantic Ocean, twice. He has consistently put himself in the way of genuine life-threatening situations that create fear, and for longer than seems humanly possible. This is him recounting one of the hardest days of his second crossing, which he did solo:

> A massive wave crashed over the boat, taking the rear up, until it felt as if the boat was going to flip over. Using the length of the boat – 22 feet – as a yardstick, it must have been 50 foot high. The last 10 foot, as it was breaking over itself, felt almost like a solid wall of water. I thought, this is it. I'll be unbelievably lucky to get out of this.

Put yourself in Lee's place, totally alone, in the middle of a huge ocean, in a storm. This is how he describes the feeling:

> Fear seeps into every part of your being, every part of your mind. Every thought, every emotion is tinged with fear, almost like a sponge sucking up water until it can't suck up any more.
>
> Time slowed down. I started to think of my next step, to plan. If the boat flipped, how I was going to get

out of it? How was I going to deal with nearly a ton of boat landing on top of me? I'm attached to it by a strap. I thought how to reach my knife so, if that happened, I could cut my way out. I thought of the second little knife I had attached to my life jacket. Then I thought: that's a last resort. Don't be too quick to cut, because if you detach from the boat, you're dead. You're on your own in the middle of an ocean in a storm, with no way back.

All this was going through my mind in an instant, and then the wave broke and the boat kind of surfed down it. My right oar had dug in and I was desperate to get it out to avoid the boat going side on to the wave because then I'd roll. I had to get the oar free.

I did it, but while my attention had been on that right oar, my left oar had dipped in too and had begun to turn me back. When I got down off that wave it wasn't over, I was still in very rough seas. The waves were deep valleys, big cliffs and they kept coming. But it is the wave that breaks on you that is trouble.

The first time Lee rowed the Atlantic, he did it as part of a four-strong team of disabled ex-servicemen. But being alone, he said, was much harder. It left a gap that allowed the fear to get in. 'It was definitely different being scared on my own rather than when I was part of a team.'

It meant he had to be creative to find ways to deal with the fear:

I had to come up with a new coping strategy. I began to save up little morsels of morale. When I reached one of my favourite songs on my playlist or a page-turning moment in an audio book, I'd mark it. If I pulled out my rations for the day and it was one of my favourite foods, fruit or, one day, a tin of peaches, I'd hide it away. Then, when I was petrified, I'd distract myself with them.

The loneliness made the trip tougher too, Lee says:

About two weeks out from finishing, my plan was to hit a particular south-to-north current that runs up the coast of South America. I needed it to push me up into where I was finishing, so it was quite critical that I got it right.

The calculation was based on me rowing 40 to 50 miles a day. At that point, I hit the wall. I had nothing left to give, mentally or physically. But I had to keep on rowing or I would miss the current and end up too far up. Slowing down wasn't an option.

The mental gymnastics I had to do to get myself out there every rowing shift were horrific. I became physically exhausted, then mentally exhausted, then emotionally too. I no longer could feel why I was doing it. I was thinking, "What's the point"? I rang Scotty [Major Scott Mills – a friend and colleague] off the cuff for a chat and he started telling me how proud he was of me. How I'd stuck my head above the parapet, and how much support there was for me. I broke down crying, in a good way. I needed that release.

As you've heard, Lee knocked 36 days off the able-bodied solo world record.

Prepared for anything

Like Lee, your task is to deny fear any room, time or space by creating a plan and following it religiously. This is no time for spontaneity, changing your mind or half-hearted maybe-maybe-not choices.

Elite athletes treat their fear- and anxiety-management routines the same way as any other part of their programme. The idea is to plan what you have to do, then rehearse the hell out of that plan until it becomes second nature.

Of course, you can't always predict when fear will freak you out. Sometimes you simply have to wing it. That might be late at night, when you turn a corner and walk into a gang of jeering strangers, faces hidden under hoodies. Or maybe you're in a bar, and you sense trouble is about to kick off. Or you're in an almost empty train carriage and a guy is staring at you.

The way you deal with those situations is not so different from being, for example, a footballer taking a penalty. The player will know they may have to take a penalty, but they won't know it's definite, or exactly when it might happen. You could even argue that it's better to be thrown into a situation than to have a long build-up.

The good news is that the more you've practised the fear management techniques shown below, the more likely it is you'll be able to think, to choose to act rather than let fear take over. That will allow you the space to work out if the stranger on the train is really a threat or not. Or to remember your driving test examiner isn't trying to catch you out, just doing her job. Or to know that you've memorised every word of your speech.

Whether or not you're expecting to be scared, if you have practised your routine, you know you'll be able to handle whatever comes up.

Three pressure strategies

When you face a moment of critical pressure, you have three main approaches for dealing with your fear: Process it (engage in a routine that gets it under control), Distract from it, or Rationalise it (use logic to overcome it).

You'll find what works for you by trying them out. I've known players to have two or three or even more approaches in their personal toolkit. For example, one might process fear with a breathing routine and also by rationalising it. Another will both rationalise and distract herself. And once you've found what works for you, it's very comforting to know you can take back control over your mind.

1. Process it

You can wrest back a degree of control as soon as fear comes up by immediately performing a deliberate and active routine. The player taking a penalty may feel the gripping in their stomach, the rush of fear. But they have to put the ball on the spot and get on with their job. It's not helpful to hang around with the fear, giving it time to take over. Instead, fear has to be immediately 'bossed', put back in its box.

That could be with a breathing routine, visualisation, affirmation or a relaxation process. Whatever routine you choose, do it immediately. The key is to act straight away, no time wasted, just act. Because a gap will allow fear to slither in.

If in doubt, start with your breathing. When you're scared, you tend to breathe shallowly and fast, trapping the air in your throat and chest, denying your tense muscles the oxygen they need and tightening up every sinew. You can physically counter fear with controlled, measured breathing.

You might think changing your breath is too simple to be powerful. In fact, your breath is your number one ally for staying in the moment. Fear doesn't like the dopamine or the ease that comes with a cool, deep breath. When you have a steady breath and body awareness, it is a lot harder to be dragged into the mental chaos that fear prefers.

An instructional physical routine might go like this. Say to yourself: 'I drop my shoulders, put my head up, I open my back and chest with a deep inhale, I put all four corners of my feet on the ground, I unclench my jaw, I release my tongue from pressing on the roof of my mouth, I release the muscles in my thighs, in my back, in my shoulders, in my neck.'

It's hard to be overtaken by fear while you're actively releasing tension, just like it's hard to clench your fist and shake hands at the same time. If you put your attention where you want it, you can use the energy of fear in a way that serves you, rather than allowing yourself to become caught up in a slipstream of negativity, fear and doubt.

Words are powerful, too. The right affirmation will boost your confidence, ground you in positivity, change the tone of what's in front of you, and make fear seem less relevant.

Whatever words you choose, it has to sound true to you. Feel free to adapt these examples: 'We've done this 10,000 times. Nothing new here, my friend, just another play'; 'Cool head, soft face, easy movements'; 'I stay persistent and positive'; 'I have succeeded in this kind of situation many times'; 'There is nothing that can happen that will make me less of a person'.

Or, in your head, you might talk to the fear: 'I recognise you. I can feel you flipping my stomach over. Settle down. We've got time. Breathe. I've got this covered. We're all right.'

This kind of soothing stops fear from telling you that you aren't ready or you might not have what it takes. You're speaking over the top of the intrusive babble coming from the fear-driven part of your mind.

One mantra I particularly like is, 'Gratitude for this opportunity', because it quickly switches you away from risk and fear, back to possibility and ambition. If you spend time considering how fortunate you are to be standing with the ball at your feet or talking to this crowd or taking this test, it will come more easily.

Some people find they can transcend the fear experience by saying the result has been taken out of their hands, surrendering to fate, God or the universe. This might be with prayer, if this is your thing. Or it could be rubbing a lucky coin, or touching a special necklace.

2. Distract from it

Often we do better when we don't think about what is scaring us. Just as Lee did, you can deliberately choose to focus your mind away from the fear. Alone on the ocean, his tins of fruit, saved favourite pages and songs were a creative solution to what he admits was a pretty tough time.

Distraction is useful when you can't rationalise fear. Instead you can simply take yourself out of the emotion.

Some ways of distracting yourself might be to put on music, to chat about unrelated subjects to the nearest person, or to watch a favourite programme.

You'll see this in the changing room before a game. Some players wear headphones and are in their own zone. Others are play-fighting and bantering, talking about what they saw on YouTube last night.

Teammates, for example, might exchange words and make each other laugh when they are waiting to take a penalty. Or if you're going to take your driving test, you might get a moment of distraction and reassurance when your dad gives you a wink and makes you laugh before you drive away.

The downside to distraction is that it is temporary. But it works well as one strategy among many when you have to tolerate fear for an extended period of time. You'll notice that Lee Spencer was combining distraction with rewarding himself too, as well as rationalising, and connecting with others.

3. Rationalise it

In critical moments, you can tackle fear with logic.

For example, if you hit strong turbulence on a flight and the oxygen masks drop, you might start to think, 'We're going to crash!' Using your rational mind allows you to create distance between you and the fear. Start to consider it logically. Even if other people are panicking around you, you can keep your mind on what has been proven. And that is: the probability of a plane crashing is, in fact, very low. And that of a safe landing is extremely high.

Perhaps one of the most extraordinary embodiments of using logic and the power of the mind to overcome fear is New Zealander William Trubridge.

William is the current free-diving world champion and an 18-times world record holder. A free-diver has to descend – on a single breath – to the deepest, darkest depths that they can tolerate physiologically and psychologically before turning to make the dangerous ascent back to the surface.

In July 2016, William dived at the world's deepest marine cavern, Dean's Blue Hole in the Bahamas. During a dive of four minutes and 14 seconds, he propelled himself with just his arms and legs down to 102 metres (335 feet). That's twice the length of the Statue of Liberty.

He'd failed before in 2014, so his success was by no means a certainty:[5]

> On the way up I started to feel a little bit of a fade about halfway; the sense of an urge to breathe and hypoxia (low oxygen) coming on, and I started to wonder whether it was going to go pear-shaped again. I just tried to kind of stay relaxed and focused and that sensation didn't get any worse, which is good.

For most of us, just the thought of being that deep in the sea, taking part in a sport that is considered the second most dangerous in the world after BASE jumping,[6] would be beyond terrifying.

Some high-profile divers have lost their lives. But William says that isn't what worries him. 'In free-diving itself there is very little that scares me,' he says. 'I see the risk as a calculated one that's quite minimal in cases where we are training with adequate safety or in competitions.' He says he becomes way more worried about driving his family, even an everyday journey, because the risk comes from other drivers, so it can't be prepared for or predicted.

As I wrote in chapter 6, your mind makes it easy to sway towards fear and negativity. But, like William, you can make a choice of considering whatever's happening in terms of possibilities, not risks. We only have a finite amount of attention; use it deliberately. He's clinically rational about the risks and the safety measures:

> People often ask me, what would you do if something happened at depth? If you were down there by yourself? What if something goes wrong? When I consider that, I can't come up with any scenarios that aren't provided for that have any degree of probability. Although there are obviously freak things that can happen.
>
> In free-diving, the water is the same at the surface as it is at depth. The only other variable is yourself. You are completely in control. You can provide for the risks that you know about. People think what I'm doing is on a death wish or is kamikaze, but if anything it's the exact opposite.

If something bad does happen, staying logical will allow you to consciously work out a strategy. Imagine you answer the phone to hear that a loved one has been injured. It would be easy to leap into catastrophic thinking, your mind jumping to the worst-case scenario. Or you could move to a plan of action: Can you get to the hospital? What is the best way? And if not, who can get there? Who else should you call?

Another way of tackling *in-the-moment* fear is to reframe it, tell yourself that it is actually just a sign of your physical readiness and engagement – something to feel good about. You can rename butterflies as excitement rather than dread.

This obviously won't apply to being mugged or getting into a fight, but it does apply to playing sports and to speaking in public (although you may not believe this as you stand up, knees shaking). This is why it is so important to stay tuned in to your body rather than just be in your head. That allows you to observe, witness, acknowledge it, then reframe it.

After all, you've probably enjoyed the thrill of fear before. It's why we like fairground rides or bungy-jumping from an outrageous height. When you know fear is manageable, it's going to pass, you're safe and there are boundaries, it becomes bearable – and therefore the choice to do those things is rational.

Some people can use fear to their advantage or as part of coping, when there are boundaries. I worked with a lawyer, a high-achieving rising star, who from the outside looked incredibly capable. But every time she knew she had to stand up in a courtroom, fear clouded her mind, she'd overthink and get overexcited and dramatic feeling like she was not preparing well.

When we dug down to what resulted in her best performance, we worked out that this mini-crisis was absolutely part of her build-up and preparation. She felt she needed to go through this to give her best and get most of her 'neurotic' emotion out.

What worked was for her to put two boundaries around it. 1) She wouldn't let the drama turn negative with self-criticism or denigrating self-talk ('you are too stupid to do this'). And 2)

She needed to stop the drama 48 hours before she went to court, otherwise it would be too tiring.

So although it seems irrational that she allowed herself to engage with her fear, to be the opposite of calm, the limits put her in control.

There's another use for 'safe' forms of fear, in for example, horror films. They are a way of people practising being scared, according to Søren Birkvad, Associate Professor in Film and Television Studies at Inland Norway University:[7]

> We see it in the way teenage boys occasionally use horror films as part of a kind of manhood test where it is about keeping one's composure as much as possible. In this perspective, the horror film becomes a way to test our personal and collective limits in a safe environment. If it gets too scary, you can just cover your ears, put your hands in front of your eyes, ease the tension with an amusing quip, or turn to your popcorn bowl for comfort.

Something similar happens for fans at key moments in sport. If you look at a football stand just before a player takes a penalty, you'll see the fans will have their hands to their faces and their eyes wide – something like the expression of the pale figure in Edvard Munch's *The Scream*.

If you've been in that crowd you'll know that, at that moment, despite the thousands of people, there's pin-drop silence. It can feel as if you're about to take the kick yourself. You can't move even to sip your drink or eat a single chip. It isn't merely butterflies, it feels like real fear. This is what you came for. You wait for the strike, the seconds dragging out.

Afterwards, people say, 'My heart was in my mouth' or 'My stomach was churning'.

Again, the key is that you know the fear will end. You might not have ever consciously watched a movie or a game to practise being scared, but by doing this, you've showed yourself that you can bear fear and that the fear will end.

Free-diver William Trubridge has a rationalising technique called 'Nerves Aren't Real' that you could try. He developed it after realising that, while diving, his nemesis is not a fear of the actual dive or the pressure or the pain, but a fear of failure. In a competition attempt, he says, failure of the dive will normally mean blackout, on the surface or just below it. But even with a blackout, he'd still have enough oxygen for minutes of brain supply, and be rescued. 'So it's less the danger of a blackout than the wounded pride of failure that drives anxiety prior to the dive.'

He recognises that most of what we fear is a projection of what might happen in the future and not something that is happening right now. And that it may never happen. This is how he describes using the technique during a dive:

> When I felt the fluttering sensation that heralds this
> anxiety I didn't shy away from it, but rather looked
> for a concrete source in the present moment, and when
> I couldn't find one it was further confirmation that
> nerves aren't real. Gradually, rather than being at the
> mercy of these nerves, I was able to keep them in
> control and brush them aside with a cursory thought:
> 'nerves aren't real'.

When his fear wasn't in the mood to be labelled 'not real', William had a second rationalisation technique ready, called The Other Extreme. Instead of trying to minimise his fear of failure and embarrassment, he ramped it right up. He imagined that people would die if he didn't succeed. 'What if my life or the lives of others actually did depend on the outcome? What if it was imperative that I was successful? When compared to those kind of stakes, the fear of simply being embarrassed is laughable.'

He didn't let himself get sucked into this catastrophic thought. Rather, he says, 'I entertain the idea for just long enough to put in perspective just how frivolous this circus-style record attempt really is. How silly I was for letting something so trivial affect my emotional state.'

More ideas for processing fear

There are many techniques for processing *in-the-moment* fear, but I've included these ones from William because they are so powerful. I've included ways you might want to adapt them to suit you.

1. **Now is all.** William says that in his sport – as in life – it's easy to get caught up in what-if thinking, where your mind can take you into unwanted drama. You are not your thoughts, and a lot of your fear-filled thoughts are simply rubbish you habitually recycle. It is impossible to do that if you are only in the present moment. William gets there by focusing on his breathing and using a mantra. 'The idea is, you have these words with powerful

connotations so they can very quickly get you into the necessary state,' he says.[8] One he often uses is: 'Now Is All'. You'll likely have to repeat the words you choose again and again while you breathe easily and steadily, in order to make this new habit take the place of your thoughts being hijacked by negativity. You could choose any word or combination that works for you: try 'positive', 'breathe', 'open', 'free', 'ready', 'confident' or 'content'.

2. **Shut down**. This is another mantra William has used – this time, to trigger his whole self into relaxation. 'For a long time, when I wanted to relax as deeply as possible, as I descended and reached the free-fall stage of the dive and was able to stop swimming, I'd give myself the mental command: "shut down". The idea was to trigger all the muscles of the body to relax as well as a deep mental state of relaxation.'[9] You could try doing this during meditation or when you're relaxed in bed. Again, you can use whatever word or words you want to associate with that feeling; try 'calm', 'peaceful', 'relaxed' or 'let go'.

3. **All of me**. Most of us walk around as if we were just brains on legs and spend all of our attention in the mind. We don't fully taste, smell, feel, see or listen – including listening to our gut instincts. For his best performance, William says he needs all elements of the self on board; the body, mind, what

he calls the 'under-mind' (subconscious) and the spirit (the driver or inner fire that pushes him on). To do this, during training and before a dive he addresses each of these in turn. You can do the same: speak to each of these parts of you as if they are a part of your team and let them know you are about to need all of their resources.

4. **Orange Light**. William adapted this visualisation from Qi Gong. As you make specific hand movements, imagine creating a ball of energetic light. Then you imagine storing it in the space between the navel and the perineum, considered to be the seat of the body's energy in martial arts. The ball acts as a reserve source of power that you can access in difficult circumstances, both for *in-the-moment* fear and any other fear triggers. What this meant for William is that during a world record attempt, he knew he'd have this extra energy available, if needed. 'Do I believe in such an energy? Not literally. But I do believe in the psychological effects that this kind of visualisation can have. If nothing else, the fantasy that I had a cache of stockpiled energy ready to intervene during the dive gave me just a little extra confidence, and confidence is confidence, even when it is founded on an illusion.'[10] He made the light orange to contrast it with the blue of the ocean, but you can make yours any colour you wish.

Clear your mind

Free-diving is an extreme sport and an experimental sport because it's about pushing the physical body to its limits. But it's also an incredible example of harnessing the mind and finding out what it is capable of.

The mindset that underpins William's beyond-human aquatic feats is the absolute opposite of fear. It's the ability to truly experience each moment. I call it mental freedom. We met it in an earlier section (see page 65) on how fear limits you, and in this section there's more on how to make this mindset yours.

As you know, I separate the types of fear into *in-the-moment* and *not-good-enough* because they are best tackled in different ways. But in fact learning to be mentally free will make it easier to manage your mind in crucial moments and to recover more quickly from the deeper triggers that provoke *not-good-enough* fears too.

You can cultivate mental freedom with practice, as William does. He says he's noticed knock-on effects of his mental training in his life as well as his sport. 'I suspect it's improved my ability to have resources to confront stressful situations and stay calm. And not to be as attached to outcomes or to not engage emotionally as much.'

William understands the power of the unconscious better than just about any athlete I have met. He describes how he uses imagination to overcome fear and create mental freedom even when the body and rational mind want to rebel.

At a crucial point in a dive, called neutral buoyancy, the salt-water density becomes equal to the density of the body. Below this, your body will travel down in the water, the free-fall stage of the dive. This is the point, William says, where he needs to leave a part of himself behind – his history, hopes, regrets and worries:

> You leave behind the idea that you are terrestrial and continue with the conviction that you are aquatic . . . You see the less of yourself that you take down, the lighter you will be. Now you are in negative buoyancy. It would kill you if you did it for long enough, but at the same time it's the most beautiful part of the dive because you feel like you are being accepted and absorbed into the ocean. A terrestrial being would become more tense and agitated the deeper it descended, but that's not you. You're aquatic, remember, the ocean is your home. The deeper you merge with it, the more relaxed you become.

William describes the choice that he makes for mental freedom; that there is only the present moment, and the present self:

> It is a pretty cool place to be under the surface. Ninety-five percent of our planet's ecosystems are down there, under the water. We evolved from the ocean 530 million years ago. But it's not just our planet that has a surface layer. We have a surface boundary in our mind too, that separates the rational, conscious mind from the subconscious below. We spend most of our life above that boundary in this ethereal, untethered medium of rational thought. But meanwhile there is a quiet, deep well of subconscious. It all happens without our awareness . . . We don't know how deep it is, but we

know that things come out of it and that we've never
been to the bottom. Anyone who practises meditation or
mindfulness or even takes mind-altering substances is
taking a dive into that still sea. A hundred metres down
you can't think about politics or laundry or whether you
said the right thing. All that belongs to a different world
that you've left behind on the surface. You become
stillness.

Not only does William descend into soul territory when he
performs at this level, but he sees that we are over-reliant on
and badly trained by our busy minds, and our over-suspicious
protective egos. He emphasises how important it is to turn off
your chattering mind:

If you cannot turn off the rational, analytic mind then
neither will you be able to turn off the pestering,
pessimistic voice that shadows it. He will follow you all
the way down 'blah-blah-blahing' until you either turn
early or doom the dive through agitation and increased
oxygen consumption . . . every time you succumb to
that despairing voice, you will fuel your own fussiness
and superstition.

The extent of the fears faced by both Lee and William may
seem almost superhuman. But despite their incredible feats of
fear-busting, they are still human. To reach this level of fear-
bossing, they methodically and consistently prepare. It will
take some practice, but you can do this too.

PART 3

When fear gets distorted

CHAPTER 8

Not-good-enough fear, and how to face it

So fear is natural, and fear is central to the human experience. But when it plays out in your life in any one of its less obvious ways, it takes some work to understand what's going on below the surface.

I'm now going to guide you on a route through these types of hidden, distorted fears, called See, Face, Replace. It's not an instant fix, but searching out the ways fear is hiding in your life is a worthwhile undertaking. These distorted fears – the ones we breathe life into every day – are not only unnecessary, but a thief of our fulfilment. They're why we only win shallow.

As these fears often come in disguise, you may not recognise this as what's happening. These are some ways hidden fear might be showing itself:

Nothing you do feels enough

Fear can impede the tone and quality of any success that you experience, which I call winning shallow. Nothing ever feels quite enough, or is joyful in the way you expected. That's because you're not actually there for it; you're looking for the next mountain to climb.

You may feel agitated, have an itch for more, or want to know what's next. This kind of motivation doesn't come from authentic dreams and desires, it comes from a fear of failure, a fear that you're not enough or not doing enough, or even a fear of losing the success that you already have. Your internal experience is bland, leaving you with little room for gratitude or contentment. You're doing more status-chasing than soul-making.

You've stopped trying

Are you making excuses for not putting your whole heart into your endeavours? Is there any fear behind those excuses? You may find yourself thinking that it'd be better to have some kind of 'honourable death' than to fail. This mindset can make you accept undesirable outcomes; for example, getting injured is preferable to competing for your place than not being selected. Or you'd leave a job rather than facing feedback about your declining performance. Or end a relationship for a fake reason rather than facing the possibility of being rejected. If any of these sound familiar, it may be that fear of failure has stopped you trying to succeed.

Your relationships are suffering

If you don't want to expose your fear to others, the quality of your relationships will be reduced in both large and small ways. You may find yourself becoming overly vigilant, defensive, even bitchy, when a subject around your fear comes up or when you feel as if you might be threatened.

Another fear-based pattern in relationships is to become avoidant and withdrawing, keeping a level of distance between you and your partner, friend or family member. Or perhaps you tend to overreact with family or in your closest relationship. You feel safe enough to express your emotion – but don't explain why you feel so strongly. Or you might be clingy and overly needy. Whichever way, you find it hard to be present – here, in real time, in your relationships.

As I wrote on page 97, these are the four fear distortions I've come across most often, and they're the ones that I'm going to look at in this section.

- When you feel you have to keep yourself separate, to hide part(s) of yourself, at root you'll find your fear of being rejected.
- When you feel jealousy, at root you'll find a fear of not being lovable.
- When you get sucked into perfectionism, at root you'll find a fear of failing.
- When you want to judge people or you feel self-critical, at root you'll find a fear of inadequacy.

Remember, at the bottom of all these fears is the fear of not being good enough, of being abandoned. It is this fear – in all its distorted forms – that may be running your show.

The fear of not being good enough can surface as a vague, faceless anxiety that you can't explain or rationalise. It's when something doesn't feel right or doesn't feel enough, even while life looks great on paper.

How to uncover your *not-good-enough* fears

How can we unearth the fears that are running our lives? I've found that if we can coax them out of hiding, we can then start to change them. This is a three-stage process that I've named See, Face, Replace.

1. See it

Before you try to solve anything, it's important to see and name what it is that you're fearful of. This goes beyond self-diagnosis, labels and other people's opinions, as it's about finding a way of getting familiar with your own fears, as well as their energy and texture. What does your fear look like to you? What does it feel like? Identifying and describing your fears is the first step towards dealing with them.

2. Face it

This is when you go inwards and look at how your fear is showing up in your life. What does it cost you? What does it add to your life? What does it cost other people?

3. Replace it

Finally, you replace your fear with something that gives you more strength and hope. This comes from reinterpreting and reimagining the stories that run you. We'll get into this later.

In chapters 9 to 12, you'll read stories of people and how they have managed to See and Face all the most common fear-based behaviours. And in chapters 14 to 20, you'll find ideas from inspirational people and organisations, some of whom I've been lucky enough to meet in the course of my work, who've found powerful ways to Replace their fears. None of these stories are intended for you to copy exactly, rather as ways to start you thinking about your own fears and what might work for you.

In the early days of my career, I provided talking therapies to my clients. Most of my work was within what you'd traditionally think of as therapy, talking to people about how they felt and their experiences, and using psychological explanations, diagnoses, labels and cognitive models to support the work. And I still find these useful today. But I have realised there's another well of resources available to us in finding real, sustainable solutions for dealing with emotions. This is using the wisdom of your own body and mind, especially your imagination.

Over years of coaching and counselling conversations, I've found going beyond reason and rationality, tapping into the imagination, to be a powerful complement to traditional talking therapies. The imagination gives us little nuggets of wisdom that come in the form of images and stories about what is going on for us. They can add useful layers to our understanding, give us some clues about what is hiding inside. So as much as you want to 'fix' your feelings and transform immediately, sometimes giving a little bit of space to the imagination is useful.

Bringing images into play might take a little longer than using labels or words to try to see and describe your fear. But it is also much richer and offers us many more insights. It's the kind of 'seeing' that you add to bit by bit, the way a piece of art gets created, in layers. And I've found that slower change with these more vivid insights is better, the kind of change that lasts.

Below, I'm going to explain what using images looks like, and the stories in chapters 14 to 20 will bring it to life for you too. There is no work I do now that doesn't have this at the root of it.

You might associate your imagination with creating fear – the imagination running wild, an overactive imagination. Which might explain why it's been ignored or underused. But it's equally powerful as a way of understanding. As author Deepak Chopra wrote,[11] 'The best use of imagination is creativity. The worst use of imagination is anxiety.'

1. See your fear

We can start by looking for openings in our life that let in unnecessary, distorted fear – particularly in our relationships and environments. The idea of the 'seeing' stage is to understand the many faces of fear and the force of energy or feeling-texture that goes with them. The idea is for you to see your fear, but also feel it, experience it, acknowledge how it plays out.

To do this, you can describe your fear by using language, logic, labels and all the things you might be familiar with, but you can also use all the information and wisdom that's already contained in your brilliant imagination. I've found that asking questions that help people to bring up an image for their fear is incredibly useful.

Images add texture to what we are trying to explain. Let me offer a couple of examples using other emotions: if your partner said your anger tears at their skin 'like rusty fish hooks', you'd experience the tone of their emotion so much more than if they said, 'I'm angry'. As well as the pain from the hook, you get the feeling that the rust could infect the wound and be even more deadly. You can start to see the hurt and worry your partner experiences when you are angry.

Or, you might describe your frustration at hearing your friend complain constantly about her terrible ex-partner as feeling like a blister between your toes that rubs and stings so much you can't ignore it. It's not just mildly annoying, it is stingingly irritating. This communicates not only the strength of your irritation, but it suggests a sense of urgency. It conveys that you need to do something about it but you're not sure whether you should 'pop the blister' and be honest about your rising intolerance or just wait and hope it goes away on its own.

Fear is an energy, and if we try to use only words to articulate it, it can lose some of what we want to express, like pouring it into a jar that is too small: a lot of the meaning will run down the sides. The words we might choose often come from other people too, whereas images are more likely to be just your own.

When you use an image, it's vivid and comes from your soul. It lets you get a little closer to the experience of fear itself, nestled in your unconscious.

And you already use images to describe emotions. For example, is the show-off in you 'overinflated'? Is the loud-mouthed guy over there 'too big for his boots'? Is your kid the 'apple of your eye'? Was the drama at work a 'storm in a tea-cup' or a 'mountain out of a molehill'?

You may find these questions help you find your images:

- What does the fear feel like? For example, is it tight and bound up? Does it erupt like a volcano? Does it creep like a spider?
- Where do you feel it in your body? Is it in your throat, choking you? Is it in your legs, lead-like? Is it in your guts, churning?
- If it had a texture, what might that be? Is it spiky, rough, slimy, hardened?
- What temperature comes with it? Is it burning, freezing, tepid, icy?
- What kind of energy comes with it? Is it biting, ripping, stinging, flattening, smothering, scalding?

If you can think of an image for it, what might that be? Maybe something in nature: you're standing on the edge of a raging river breaking its banks, sliding on mud with no sure footing? Stumbling through a pitch-black forest at night? Confronted by a snarling dog? Being trapped underwater?

Can you hear the tone of the fear and feel how each one is different? The river suggests feeling out of control. The forest suggests feeling lost and in the dark, unable to navigate. The snarling dog suggest feeling under attack. Being underwater suggests panic.

When I begin asking questions along these lines, people are often confused. But once they get started, it's amazing how quickly they find their image. Your imagination might be underused but it is a powerful ally.

Of course, language is also mighty. But I've found that when using only logic and words, people can stay superficial. They can also sometimes blame an *in-the-moment* fear, when running underneath it is a *not-good-enough* fear. For example, you may fear making a speech. You may rationalise that this is because you'll forget your words. But the distorted fear that's really running the show is that you will be rejected for being not good enough.

Images give us a window into our unconscious, the part of us that isn't our reasoning brain. And the unconscious is a vastly underused resource, powerful in helping us tap into the emotions and energies of our lives.

Our unconscious used to be thought of as a dark and vast realm of mysterious instincts and drives. More recently, it's been revealed to be a wonderland of powerful psychological capabilities. It's working all the time via our judgements, predictions, feelings, stories and motives. But because its capacity hasn't been understood, we haven't always used its capability to help us understand ourselves better.

What I'm suggesting will likely sound alien to you. We are so used to operating in the realm of logical thoughts, concepts and theories, not just in therapy but in life too. As Thomas Moore, author of the bestseller *Care of the Soul*, says: 'The world we live in tends to see the world mechanistically or physically alone. They don't understand that there is some invisible dimension to our experience. To everything. Even to nature. And so we tend to reduce things too much.'

We are usually so wound up in logic and facts and evidence that we turn a blind eye to what else we feel, in our guts, in our hearts, in our imagination and in our unconscious. These ways of knowing are utterly valid, even if they don't directly translate to facts. And they can be a wildly powerful way of reinterpreting ourselves and our fears.

We can learn to use the unconscious via the imagination, but it's a much different way of 'thinking' than we are used to.

I worked with a New Zealand sports team as they were building an image that stood for them and their Kiwi team culture. Together, the players used their imagination to create the symbol of a sacred house. It contained their values, their beliefs, their spirit and their ancestors. There were rules that anyone who entered had to honour the house, and therefore the team. There were rituals to welcome newcomers and rituals to say goodbye to old friends.

To the outsider, the house itself might have only existed in the team's imagination, but it had an energy that was separate to any individual, and a presence that was to be respected. There were carvings on the wooden columns that held up the house that told the story of 'their way'. The house was so far beyond a metaphor, it was a powerful behavioural driver – even though it was created with not one present-day fact, piece of evidence or logic.

This shows how the unconscious gives you a way into deeper meaning and emotion, to connection and belonging. It gives value to things that were not visible: their ancestral history, the people who wore the shirt before them, the sanctity of their culture.

In the same way, you can access the deeper meaning of your *not-good-enough* fears when you bring in your imagination. You can start to access 'what might not be visible' at first glance to you.

As well as asking yourself questions, you can help reveal the energy of your fear by noticing it in your body and mind, when it comes up. Make the decision that you're no longer going to hide your fears or cover them or push them down before you take a look.

When you start to look at your deeper fears, instead of being on autopilot, notice how you change when you're in a particular environment. Make time to reflect quietly, as this will give your fears the space to surface and be seen. You can also help them take shape, when they come up, by speaking them out loud to trusted people or even noting them down.

Don't rush this. It needs self-compassion, space and time. If you jump to an 'A-ha' solution, it will feel good for three days or three weeks, then the fear will slime its way back in. But give it time, and you'll begin to find images to describe what you feel in a way that will stick with you.

I've talked about behavioural signs that could indicate your fear, but your body will communicate too. Your body and mind are not so separate.

You may feel dull and withdrawn in a particular environment, so your body feels heavy and your energy isn't flowing easily. Or your energy may be scattered, so you're jumping from one thing to another, texting, browsing, working, talking, driving.

Your sluggishness, your feeling of being drained, or having a grumbling stomach. What do you think your body is telling you about your emotional state? Stop and listen to it for a moment.

The more you give attention to how you feel, the more you stay open to images and the more you notice who or what triggers you into *not-good-enough* fear and what it feels like, the more chance you have of really addressing it.

2. Facing your fear

Once you have seen your *not-good-enough* fear, then you face it. This means rather than turning away from it, you go deeper in to it. This is the hardest part.

Of course, fear will feel horrible. So it's a no-brainer that you'll want to shut it off as quickly as possible. The problem is, shutting it down won't work if you want to change these pervasive, distorted forms of fear. Fear is dogged. Avoiding it and denying it only give it more energy.

It is only through being present with your fear that you can see how it's operating in your life, what it wants and what you might do about it. By admitting how your fear is playing out in your life, you will see it taking shape. You will notice how it affects your relationships and your choices.

You might see where fear hinders you and even where it is useful. Look at where it spills out and affects other people. And look at where it steals your ambitions and dampens your passions.

Asking these questions may help you do this:

Who do I become when I am captured by fear?

Who in me gets squashed when fear arrives?

When fear arrives, what changes in my relationships?

When fear arrives, what changes in my behaviour, my mood, my energy?

Where does fear make me want to quit?

What does fear stop me cultivating or growing?

What would I have to leave behind if I let go of this fear? (what excuses, what reasons, what stories, what identity)

Would letting go clear the path for what I want?

How might my life be different if I took out this fear? How would I expand?

What does my fear cost me?

What does my fear cost the people around me?

What excuses does my fear make for me?

What attitudes and beliefs do I have that help keep my fear alive?
What about the culture I'm in keeps my fear thriving?
What of my passions and ambitions is fear keeping me away from?

There are a lot of questions here. You don't need to ask them all, but going deeper into fears will undoubtedly take time. And be warned: it won't be all positive and pretty. It will require some courage, truth and soul-searching on your part, as well as endurance. You may feel stuck in the darkness for a while. But as the poet Theodore Roethke wrote: 'In a dark time, the eye begins to see.'

It might mean admitting uncomfortable things to yourself, such as:

I don't want to be here but I'm afraid of being a failure if I walk out.
I am afraid of looking like an idiot in front of them and it is making me avoid speaking up.
I am afraid that it will all happen again if I try.
I'm afraid that I won't be able to bear the pain.
I am terrified that if I turn this down, there won't be another chance.
I am afraid I won't have the strength for this and I'll crumble in shame.
What if everyone knows I'm not really good enough.

The idea of facing fear can be overwhelming – will you be able to deal with the pain? Will you have the courage you need to overcome it? Who will you be if you let go of the way you cope with life today? What are you prepared to see – and what are you prepared to let die off as a result?

Trust in yourself, know you are resilient, remember who you are. Excavating your fears and saying them out loud is like bleeding the trapped air from your radiators. It will allow the energy of your life to start moving freely. And when this happens, you'll be able to take the next step.

3. Replacing your fear

Finally, the objective is to create more mental freedom. You'll do this by replacing your *not-good-enough* fears with solid alternative narratives, mindsets and decisions.

What you uncover as you are starting to See and Face your *not-good-enough* fears and how they impact you and those around you won't be wasted. It is growth material. In nature, when organic matter decays, it becomes part of the nutrients for new growth. The same is true of your fears.

To make this happen, you'll need to make a deliberate effort to kill off the fear-based stories that are running you. Whenever there is a *not-good-enough* fear, there is a story built up around it that you have taken on as true about you not being enough as a human being in some way, not being really lovable, if people only knew the truth about you. These narratives are penned and perpetuated between you and the culture you live in, but it is only you who can decide if they are true or not. Once you've seen what you are afraid of, you've faced how it is showing up in your life and what it is costing you, you have created some space for possible alternative stories to underpin your life; stories about who you are, your resilience and your potential. It is these stories you tell yourself and others, the stories that run you, that set the tone of your life.

This is what Part 4, chapters 14 to 20, is about, to show you the different ways people have transformed the fear that is holding them back, and to give you ideas on how to change your life. Because it is possible to replace your fear with something that gives you strength and hope and allows for more fulfilling connections with your fellow man. You could describe this as a re-story — telling how it is for you, but in a new way. This is how not to lose yourself while you're winning at life.

Real stories of fear

The next four chapters, chapters 9 to 12, are about how *not-good-enough* fears play out in the lives of real people.

These stories are woven together from the professional and private conversations that I have had over 20 years. They also include stories generously shared by professional colleagues and friends. Those who were courageous enough to tell their stories have had their details changed to protect their confidentiality.

After each story, there are examples of the kinds of conversations that I might use to See and Face the energy of fear. These are to help you reflect on what stories are running you and how fear shows up in your life. You'll see that what each of these people has done in uncovering their *not-good-enough* fear is brave, but so worthwhile.

CHAPTER 9

Distorted fear: staying separate

It's normal to wear a mask some of the time. You're likely to be different at work or with people you have just met to how you are with old friends or family. It's also natural to prefer to be private, or to have an introvert's reserve.

But staying separate is distinct from any of these. This chapter describes what happens when you pretend to be who you aren't because you want to keep some part of yourself hidden from other people. And you do this because you fear that if people saw the real you, they would not accept you. It's feeling unable or unwilling to expose your flaws, or reveal what you see as unacceptable about yourself.

What might this look like in your life? One clue that you're afraid of showing yourself fully could be that you avoid certain social groups, friends or family members. Or it could be you don't want to introduce your partner to your colleagues. Put simply, you don't want some people to see other parts of your life or you.

There are lots of other ways people keep themselves separate too. It could be you prefer not to share something about your origins, for example your race or class or the fact you were adopted. Or that you have a criminal record, or a criminal in your family. Or that you didn't finish school or go to university. I've met more than a few professional athletes and others who don't want people to know they can't read well.

This may seem old-fashioned, but another common piece of themselves that people keep hidden is around sexual history, whether it's that the person fears they'd be judged or rejected because they've slept with too many people or too few. You might not want to reveal the fact you've been divorced, especially if it's more than once. Or that you've had cosmetic treatments – Botox or lip-fillers – but don't want others to know.

I think that all of these things are fine in themselves. And it's also fine not to tell everything. We all hide large and small parts of ourselves. Hiding things is only the first step to separateness. The vital question, which will tell you if fear is at the root, is: would you feel shame if what you are hiding was exposed?

If the answer is yes, there is a massive cost to keeping parts of yourself hidden. The effort required to stay separate from other people is a serious drain on your well-being and happiness.

If you dig down into this shame, what you'll find is a fear of being exposed, then rejected. This fear can be corrosive, in that it can eat away at your sense of identity and worth, leaving you feeling like a fraud. The story below is about an athlete who didn't want to tell people he was gay. He felt he couldn't come out because he would be judged and rejected, and he couldn't see beyond the shame he felt about being gay, or what he thought his teammates and family would feel about his sexuality.

The ultimate cost of staying separate because you are afraid to be fully seen is a cost to your ability to experience and give love. You can't keep love between you and another person in a private space – mental or physical – and hope it will still nourish you. The flame of it, however strong, needs oxygen to survive, as you'll see from Jake's story below. Love is not just a relationship with someone, it is a way of living life fully.

'I couldn't tell anyone that I'm gay'

This is the story of Jake, a successful athlete whose shame of being a gay man, and his fear of rejection, affected his relationship with his family, friends and teammates, and led him to lead an increasingly isolated life:

> I've always been a private person. I'm not shy, in fact I can be pretty loud. But I don't like anyone to be in my business and I hate people who get nosy. I don't trust anyone, not even most of my family. They are all sharks. They all want something from me. And I don't get close to anyone at the club. Actually, I don't get close to anyone, anywhere.
>
> I know I'm living a lie. But if I told the truth, can you imagine what would happen at the club? And with the media and the fans? There's no way I want to be the poster boy for being gay in my sport.
>
> I've worked really hard to get my chance. There is only a small amount of time you get to play the

game at this level. I want to make the most of it without hearing about being a faggot every five minutes.

Recently, I was doing some media and this female interviewer was asking way too many personal questions, what I like in a girl and so on. I went into what I call my 'fake-Jake' mode and made up all sorts of crap. You should have heard me (laughs).

Every single person at school and the club knows me as fake-Jake. Even Mum and Dad. When I was a kid, we were really close. Now, they probably think I'm ungrateful because most of the time I stay away from them. They are so proud of me and my career that they have put me on a pedestal. So, if they found out, it would be a big fall. I cringe when I think how disappointed they would be about me lying to them all this time, let alone about not being straight.

When I was 19, I had a bust-up with a cousin. He was teasing me and he called me gay. I saw red because I thought his big mouth was about to expose me. So I smacked him one. My overreaction surprised everyone, even me.

I spend a lot of my time and energy listening to the voice in my head telling me I'm a fraud and a loser. I'm not crazy, I just don't feel comfortable with being gay and I don't think others would be comfortable with it either.

I'm always thinking I'm going to be found out. When I started at this club, I had a girlfriend for a couple of years. I was trying really hard to be straight but I'm just bent (laughs).

It sounds as if I was using her, but I wasn't. She was a decent person, and I really wanted to feel normal and to fit in. She always said I was moody and closed-off, that I needed to 'open up'. She wanted more attention from me but I didn't have it to give.

I'm paranoid, but sometimes I think, deep down, she knew. But she never said anything and for that I'm grateful. I don't know what I would have done if she'd got me at a weak moment, especially near the end of our relationship. There was lots I liked about being with her, mostly everyday things such as hanging out. And I liked seeing my parents happy about it. I talked myself in to us being real, that we had a future together.

It was the best time for me in my career because I didn't stress so much. If anyone was being nosy about my day off, I could shut them down by saying a couple of things about her, then get on with training. On game day, I didn't have any extra stress on my mind. When I was invited to awards nights and club family days, it was much easier to have a girlfriend with me.

For a couple of years, we bobbed along OK but then she started to talk about babies and marriage. When I thought about how big my lie had got, it made me feel physically sick with fear.

I began to avoid her. The more I did this, the more she thought I was having a fling with another woman – ha! When I wouldn't commit, she got more and more agitated. She kept asking whether I loved her. How was I supposed to answer that? I did, I really did, but not in the way she needed.

She stopped trusting me. She became cold and then a bit mean too. I felt as if I was really letting her down but I couldn't even give her a reason for why I was acting the way I was.

I felt trapped but also very lonely in that relationship. When she finally broke it off, I felt conflicted: sad but also relieved.

Last year, I met a guy at a club. He didn't know what I did for a job at first, which was good. You've got to be so careful — some dickhead with a phone could take pictures without you realising and post them online. Once, when I was just starting out in my career, that happened when I was on holiday. Thank God the pictures weren't very clear and I got them taken down.

We had a relationship, of sorts. I was really sweet on him. He'd come round to my place late at night and we'd just hang out and do 'couple stuff', like sit on the sofa with the dog and watch telly and eat Nando's and have a laugh.

I felt normal for a while, or as normal as I get (laughs). I'd get excited knowing I'd be seeing him after training, had a bit of a pep in my step! But it wasn't normal, was it? It can't be normal because I was hiding and lying. I got a bit paranoid and started grilling him. I'd ask him: can you prove you're not telling anyone about me?

He started to drift away and that made me more anxious and uptight. I think I was falling in love with him. But I just kept on at him. And so I wrecked it. He said he didn't want to get dragged back into the closet because I was scared of being found out.

After that, I felt even more lost and lonely, even more separate. I wonder what I could have been if things were different. I would have had loads more energy, that's for sure! (laughs). I tried to focus on performance and distract myself from everything else. Fake-Jake kept me moving. It's all I had really, except my dog and my old mate fear. Does that sound like a lyric from a country and western song? (laughs).

Jake didn't start to work through his issues until years after his career as an athlete ended. It wasn't surprising that he didn't want to come out during his career. As I described in Part 1, there was both shame – coming from the fear of being exposed – and keeping a tight rein on what people knew about him.

Then, when his loneliness became too much for him to handle and he got into a series of bar fights, he decided to face his fear.

When I first asked Jake to begin to describe his fear, the conversation went something like this:

Pippa:	'Do you have an image for this fear, Jake? What is it like?'
Jake:	'It's just big.'
Pippa:	'Give me an image for it. What does it look like, smell like, feel like to the touch? What texture?'
Jake:	'It stinks.' (laughs)
Pippa:	'What might it be like in nature?'

Jake: 'OK, this fear was like a big and angry grizzly
             bear standing guard at the door and the chains
             around its neck and ankles were chafing and
             rubbing and hurting him, making him roar.
             There you go.'

Pippa: 'And what is the bear trying to tell you?'

Jake: 'He's trying to tell me it's not safe to go through
             the bloody door.'

Pippa: 'What is he trying to protect?'

Jake: (Sighs) 'My heart. He's trying to protect my heart.
             From pain.'

Pippa: 'Who in you feels the pain, Jake?'

Jake: (long pause) 'The 11-year-old kid feels it. Right in
             the guts. He feels ashamed in his guts.'

Pippa: 'OK. Who in you can soothe the pain for that
             11-year-old kid?'

Jake: (Long pause) 'Well, grown-up me, I guess.
             The man.'

Pippa: 'Tell me about grown-up you.'

Jake: 'Resilient. Gets things done. Funny, even if I say so
             myself. Got a softer side that cares. Loving.'

Pippa: 'What would grown-up you want to say to the
             11-year-old kid?'

Jake: (Sighs, upset) 'You're OK, kid. You're OK.'

Pippa: 'What else can he share with the kid?'

Jake: 'It's not your fault, kid.'

Pippa: 'Yes.'

Jake: 'You're not broken.'

Pippa: 'Yes.'

Jake: 'You're lovable.' (Tears, long pause) 'I'll look out
             for you.'

Pippa: 'Grown-up you will look out for the kid.'

Jake: 'Yes. I want to.'

Pippa: 'So how about the bear?'

Jake: (Shrugs) 'The bear is exhausted. He looks
          bedraggled. I think the kid wants to take his
          shackles off.'

Pippa: 'OK. Is he doing that?'

Jake: 'Yeah. The bear is settling down a bit.'

Pippa: 'Sounds like that might feel better. Jake, what is the
          story that this bear heard that meant he had to be
          so protective of the kid's heart for all this time?'

Jake: 'Well, that everyone is an arsehole and will want
          to hurt him. That everyone will reject him.'

Pippa: 'Is it true?'

Jake: 'No. Not really. Some people are good. Some
          people surprise you.'

Pippa: 'So the bear has some wrong information?'

Jake: 'Ha, yes, I guess he does. Guess he's only got part
          of the story.'

Pippa: 'What's a better narrative to give the bear, do you
          think?'

Jake: 'That it's a mixed bag out there, good and bad but
          not all bad. But he can relax a bit because I've got
          the kid by the hand.'

Pippa: 'You can take care of the kid's heart? And your
          heart? You don't need so much anger and fear?'

Jake: 'Yeah, we can look out for each other. We're fine.
          There is good stuff out there too.'

Jake had already spent years playing through his fears, trying to rationalise his insecurity and 'tell himself' to think

differently. But it wasn't until he could find ways to deal with the force of the energy that came up, by picturing it as the angry grizzly bear, that he could let go a little, then face his fear and understand how it was working.

Naming and facing his bear (his fear) was the starting point for the next stage: considering how he could 're-story' his life to feel stronger. His new story went like this: I am capable, I can nurture and care for myself, it's good and bad, but the fear doesn't need to be 'on-guard' all the time. Once Jake had these first images, he could then revisit and edit and shape them as regularly as he needed to face his fear and re-story it.

You're going to get more of a picture of ways to create this new story in chapters 14 to 20. But right now it's useful to know your new story will likely not be all peaches and cream. It will be powerful, a mixture. Jake's, for example, contains hope and positivity as well as fear. But that's what makes it more real to you, more useful.

Once Jake had named what was happening – that he was rejecting himself because he was scared that he'd be rejected by society – he was able to make the huge move of coming out to his mum and dad. It brought him to his knees with relief and pain. The three of them ended up on the kitchen floor, crying and talking for hours, sharing an old bottle of port that his mum had in the house for 'medical emergencies'. The fact that his parents were able to show him love and care at his most vulnerable both shocked him and made him feel ashamed of judging them for so long.

Jake did not choose to come out more publicly. But the renewal of and new honesty in those relationships created an extraordinary shift. He finally had enough love to let go a little and feel hope for his future.

As you read Jake's story, did any of the themes he talks about — feeling separate, lonely, not wanting people to get close or to know something about you — sound familiar? Did it remind you of any parts of you that you wouldn't want to be seen or found out? Remember, at the root of wanting to stay separate is the fear of being rejected. And the way to know if fear is behind wanting to keep something private is to ask yourself: would I feel shame if people knew that about me?

If your answer is yes, you could try rereading the See and Face sections in chapter 8. There you'll find more questions to ask yourself, to dig down into the energy of this fear.

CHAPTER 10

Distorted fear: jealousy

You know when you're hit by jealousy, it's such a forceful, frantic emotion. Jealousy lights up your amygdala, so before you can rationalise it away, your mind has reeled into action with blame, accusations and ugly words coming out of your mouth or off the tips of your texting fingers.

Sometimes jealousy is a passionate flash and goes away just as quickly. But this chapter tells the story of the kind of jealousy that's more common: when it boils over from a deeper place, a scarcity mindset that says there can only be one winner because there's not enough – love, respect, belonging, glory, accolades, rewards – to go around.

There's an even deeper root to jealousy: you are usually coming from a place of comparison and shame. It's a warning sign that you feel at risk of losing love or status in some way. It comes from the fear of not being enough, of not being loved and respected.

A jealous mind shifts your focus onto the success of other people, so it's no longer on your own possibilities and your own fulfilment. This disconnection from yourself leaves you feeling more vulnerable and less powerful than you did before jealousy hijacked you. It leaves you feeling a furious sense of lack and wanting to stem the cause of your pain. And unless you can pause and accept the vulnerability of feeling jealous for a long enough moment to listen to it, you will react.

You might have experienced how jealous behaviour can trigger a strong response in other people too, resulting in fear, need, confusion and anger ricocheting between you until something breaks, breaks down or breaks open.

One way to start dealing with jealousy is to see it as a piece of data, an uncomfortable clue to where you might need to place some of your own compassionate attention before you look deeper, face and replace your fear.

Below is the story of Caroline, a highly successful media producer in LA. The lengths her jealousy took her to are pretty extreme, as were the consequences. As you read her story, think about the last few times you felt jealous, or the times you felt most jealous. Does anything she said or did sound familiar? And is your own jealousy giving you clues about where you'll find your fear of not being loved?

'My jealousy felt like my blood boiling in the back of my head'

What I am most embarrassed about is that I took out another woman in a male-dominated industry. And I did it because I couldn't tolerate her as a threat to my own crown.

After 31 years in the TV business, when people talked about talent and quality in this genre, nine times out of ten my name would come up. I don't doubt my talent, but mostly it was down to grinding harder than anyone else and sacrificing more. I didn't tolerate anything other than 100 percent focus from myself or anyone else. I put my son in way too much after-care and too many holiday programmes, even though he didn't like them. I went through a husband and three nannies and a bucket load of bad jobs and worse bosses.

I'd been working in this particular company for six years when I offered Jess a job. At the age of 30, she was razor-sharp technically and already had a hit animation piece. She was a rising star.

Production in LA is competitive. The execs and finance control the budgets. And there's us, the creatives, who have to pitch to them for funding. I'd been at war with the execs and it often got nasty and personal. There was no love lost.

I had doubts Jess would like the way we worked. She seemed quirky and confident, not the usual type for my world, a bit too 'likeable'. But frankly, I was frothing at the mouth on what we could gain from her. With her skills on board, we could leapfrog the opposition. Jess didn't want to leave New York but I hate to lose. I eventually got her over the line, selling her the glamorous LA lifestyle combined with a salary she couldn't say no to. There were raised eyebrows all round when I announced she was coming on board as my protégé at a big price tag.

I remember the day she started, our first conversation over breakfast. I looked at her with her big brown eyes, her polka-dot blouse, drinking her almond-milk coffee, seeming like she had all the time in the world to chat. She was clearly different to me, which was mildly unsettling. But I decided she would be my girl, that I would protect her and shape her.

I told her to watch out for the bastards, that everyone had an agenda, especially the executives. And to watch out for parasites like Rob and Dion in particular, the biggest haters of all. I told her she would be fine if she stayed close to me, that I would make sure her path was cleared.

It was unheard of for me to go all-in for a kid like this. You could say I'd staked my reputation on her so I needed it to work. But even though we weren't alike, I saw something of my younger self in her. I coached her to push our ideas ruthlessly. She replied, 'I kind of like hearing other people's ideas, too.' I smiled cynically and nodded, thinking I needed to knock some of the yoga out of this one.

By month three, she was flying high and I was excited. She had a rare talent and people were noticing the crispness and quality of her outputs. Behind the scenes, I went to war with those orcs in finance to get more funding for projects to showcase her. I held back the tide of shit every day so she could perform. Now I realise she probably had no idea what I was doing. I wasn't exactly a sharer.

Six months in, walking into the building at 8 a.m., I glanced over to the coffee shop on the corner.

And I saw her sitting there, laughing away with the crustiest, meanest bastard on the executive, Rob. This was the guy who had made my life hell for six years. I hated him.

I watched them, his head thrown back in laughter, his body language open and animated as if they were deep into discussing something incredible. WTF was going on? I felt weak and clammy, then hot-mad. I had been betrayed. Why hadn't she listened to my warnings about our enemies? What were they talking about? Me?

Ten minutes later I texted Jess, demanding to see her. The first thing I said was, 'What were you doing with that asshole?'

She was taken aback but stayed composed. 'Well, Caroline,' she said, 'Rob wanted to see how I was settling in and give me some feedback on the Heiffel project.'

'What the hell has it got to do with him? You get your feedback from me,' I said, 'and it's probably best not to be seen flirting with the big boys.'

She flushed bright red and walked out. It was a low blow. But she had been disloyal.

To Jess's credit, she put her head down and pro-duced some great work on the Heiffel project, which I presented to the board a few weeks later. I had intended to take her to the meeting, but I was still agitated enough that I didn't even credit her with the work. Rob was there. He tried to pin me down several times with questions about the technical production. Eventually, he asked me outright if it was

Jess's work. On the ropes, I had to say yes. I was burning with rage.

The chairman said, 'You've chosen your successor well, Caroline. Not everyone has the leadership courage to do that, well done.'

Successor! The word sliced through me. I suddenly felt replaceable.

In an attempt to reconnect with Jess, I took her out for lunch. But in truth, I was listening for clues about her loyalties, asking questions, trying to manipulate her back to my side. She was obviously uneasy but brave enough to say she didn't feel comfortable with my questions. I admired her for that; no one ever pushed back at me. But I could also feel a twisted resentment growing in my chest.

For the next month, every time I saw people laughing with Jess, which was often, I felt the same gripping feeling in my chest. Then a client fed back that a draft piece of work Jess had done was too left-of-centre and asked for a redo. I'm ashamed to say my first emotion was glee. I was cautiously gloating about it to Jan, my long-time assistant. And she said, 'Maybe she had a hangover from Dion's party?'

I felt the blood boiling in the back of my head, heat running up my neck. In just a year, Jess was more 'in' with the power-brokers than I had been after six.

That week, I went into full power-play mode. I took Jess off a signature production, saying I felt it needed a different touch, which hurt her reputation

and her feelings. But much worse, I used the one
weapon that no woman in a man's world should: sex.
I seeded the idea around the office that she was
perhaps 'a little too friendly' with powerful people,
just enough to leave the ghost of a suggestion that she
was having an affair with one of the executives.
When people started guessing the man was Rob,
I didn't correct them.

The rumours spread like California wildfire.
Rob's wife heard them and confronted Jess in an
ugly scene. Before long, Jess was in tatters, had
packed her bags and left for the East Coast. All the
while I played it innocent. In our last conversation,
Jess said, 'Caroline: meanness doesn't make good
soil for growth for anyone.' As I feigned ignorance,
I felt childish and stupid, hating her smart-arse
composure.

Any relief was short-lived. I didn't get any more
popular. Rob, who had suffered as well as Jess,
confronted me. He said he was deeply disappointed
that a person of my position would behave like that
with any young woman, let alone one I was mentoring. Of course, I denied it all but I felt like my shame
was neon yellow and visible to all.

I wonder if it was Rob who encouraged Jess to
find a lawyer. And so began the worst year of my life.
Jess lodged and won a claim for constructive dis-
missal. She proved I had taken her down. All my
horrible behaviour was unearthed and exposed. I was
sacked by the company for misconduct. All my years
of work unravelled.

It has taken me a long time to see and admit that
what I did was driven by fear and that I wasn't just a
mean bitch, although I certainly behaved like one. I
was afraid of how much everyone liked Jess and
afraid that no one liked me. I can't tell you how hard
that is for me to say. Saying it to Jess was even harder.
She never replied to the letter, but I'm glad that at
least she knows I'm sorry.

Recognising that fear was at work underneath her jealousy
allowed Caroline to step forward and come out from under
the moral scrapheap that she – and others – had put her on.
Certainly, she behaved badly, but all behaviour makes sense
in context, even if it's wrong.

Caroline's Seeing and Facing exchanges went something
like this:

Pippa: 'You felt pretty disconnected from yourself
                through that time, Caroline?'
Caroline: 'I don't even know who I was.'
Pippa: 'Who was there beforehand? Before you were
                disconnected.'
Caroline: 'Ha! A fresh-faced and passionate creative.'
Pippa: 'Tell me about the freshness.'
Caroline: 'I was full of vision, green shoots every day. I was
                popping ideas left, right and centre. It was so
                easy back then! I was so into it, so open-minded!'
Pippa: 'What changed with that freshness?'
Caroline: 'I guess I got burned. It was a harder
                environment than I thought it was going to be, I
                was shocked. I got "put in my place" and made

	to feel dumb a few times by the executives, the big guys, and I started to feel threatened and reactive . . .'
Pippa:	'Stay with the image a while longer. What was burned?'
Caroline:	(Long pause) 'I think it was my softness.'
Pippa:	'Yes.'
Caroline:	'I chargrilled my freaking softness and femininity. Because I felt like I wasn't going to make it, I just pushed and scrapped, driving myself and hardening up until I was as hard-boiled as them. I'm shocked. I didn't even save any for my kid.'
Pippa:	'What was it that hard-boiled Caroline could offer you?'
Caroline:	'Oh that's easy. She was protection.'
Pippa:	'What else?'
Caroline:	(Quiet voice) 'She offered weapons. And I used them. In fact, I was deadly. I was toxic.'
Pippa:	'What were the weapons for?'
Caroline:	'Because I was freaking terrified I was going to be out. I thought they hated me and I wanted them to respect me. So I didn't give them a chance to get me. I started all the wars.'
Pippa:	'Who in you wrote that letter to Jess, Caroline?'
Caroline:	(Sad) 'The woman in me.'
Pippa:	'Yes.'
Caroline:	'The woman whose head isn't on fire any more.'
Pippa:	'What would that woman say to hard-boiled Caroline now?'

Caroline: (Quiet) 'I think hard-boiled Caroline has served
              her time. She is no longer required.'

Pippa: 'You can let her rest?'

Caroline: 'Yeah. I don't need to put myself under the kind
              of pressure where I need her ever again. It
              wasn't worth what I became.'

Pippa: 'OK. So you know you have a grenade-thrower
              in you when you get scared now.'

Caroline: (Smirks) 'Huh. Scared is right. Scared of not
              being liked. And exhausted. Brings out hard-
              boiled Caroline. That's where I need to pay
              attention.'

Pippa: 'That's where you want to focus?'

Caroline: 'That's what I can control and who I can be,
              yes. A calmer, softer woman who can still grow
              green shoots.'

In this exploration, Caroline isn't fabricating who she is, she's
facing who she is and what makes her feel gripped with jealousy. As the conversation goes on, you can see Caroline
coming to see and understand what happened in terms of her
fear. She isn't trying to 'fix and forget'. She's trying to focus her
attention in the most useful place, then reinterpret her behaviour and her story in a way that helps her feel strongest, most
competent and most hopeful for her future. (More detailed
ideas you can use to reinterpret – or Replace – your story are
in chapters 14 to 20.)

What's also revealing about Caroline's story is the way she
began to see how her environment provoked and added to her
fear. Operating in a ruthless, competitive workplace, Caroline
adapted so thoroughly that she completely lost herself, became

hardened, or 'hard-boiled' as she described it, even worse than everyone else she worked with.

Because Caroline saw her world as a battle against the executives, it made it devastating when her protégé was invited into their world. It heightened every particle of fear she had that she was unlovable, cast out and rejected.

Of course, jealousy can happen in any area of your life, not just work: in your relationship, friendships, with other parents, even online – especially online. As you learned in chapter 6, at the root of jealousy is the fear of being unlovable, and at the root of that is the fear of being abandoned.

When you have been jealous previously, you might have just assumed you needed to try to be less jealous. That was what Caroline assumed at first too. But that is just dealing with the surface emotion, not what's going on underneath.

The hardest part about being jealous is that it quickly crowds out your clarity. Give yourself a bit of space to let it calm down and subside before you have a better look at what was going on at that moment. Be gentle with yourself and try to not to judge yourself while you do this. It may be useful to have a look at how jealousy shows up for you more regularly too. The See and Face questions in chapter 8 will help you out here.

CHAPTER 11

Distorted fear: perfectionism

'And now that you don't have to be perfect, you can be good'

– John Steinbeck

Our culture has hundreds, maybe thousands, of role models who credit perfectionism for their podiums, prizes and plaudits. Steve Jobs, Stanley Kubrick and Maria Sharapova have all spoken up about their perfectionism. And there's no doubt that exacting standards – plus copious amounts of talent, if not genius – is what makes them great.

It's not bad to have high standards or to try your very best. But there's an important difference between that and perfectionism. At the root of the first is the desire to avoid failing, and at the root of the second is the fear of *being* a failure.

The energy of the first is all about moving towards success; the energy of the second is about running away from failure.

In my experience, the desire to avoid failing is largely motivating. It leads to things like high standards, discipline and extra effort in order to avoid mediocrity, and it also keeps your radar up for opportunities to grow and expand.

But if you are afraid you'll *be* a failure, you become weighed down rather than inspired. You see any failure as a personal flaw. Perfectionism comes with a big dose of harsh self-criticism and endless comparison and disappointment, even when you are winning at life. Fear of being a failure turns your need to get things right into a kind of oppression.

I have seen many perfectionistic high-achievers succeed. You may well be getting results from your perfectionism too. Scholars continue to play academic tennis about whether perfectionism is good or bad, functional or unhelpful. But their focus is often on whether it's good or bad for outcomes and achievements, not for the soul and fulfilment.

The question to ask yourself is: what is fuelling my perfectionism? Is it fear of failing? To be truly fulfilling, perfectionism needs to be fired up by purpose and passion (see page 211), and not by fear. Perfectionism may pull you forward; you just want to make sure it isn't by the hair.

Perfectionism, like all fear, does not like to be exposed. Try to do this and it will wriggle and repackage itself to look good and valuable. It will tell you that it is helping you to cope, that it is the reason you are going far. It won't mention that, along the way, it's also sucking the life out of you.

You'll notice how this happens in the following story: perfectionism is disguised as the only way to achieve. Emilie was an elite swimmer who, by the age of eight, was on the Olympic track, and Jacques is her perfectionist father.

'I wanted my daughter
to be no-questions-asked perfect'

I lost her. I lost my baby girl. Emilie still lives at home and I see her every day but she doesn't look me in the eye. Her smiles are fake and forced, the same one she gives someone she doesn't know well at a big family party. When I try to hug her, I can feel her body stiffen up, as if she wants to be somewhere else. Her mum says I'm overreacting and she's just being seventeen. But I know my girl.

She told her mum that I 'stole her childhood'. That kills me because she was my world. I don't know how I'll ever recover. I really love her, you know? And we can't talk about it.

I spent thousands of hours with that kid in the car, driving her to training in the sleet and snow and hail. The alarm would go off at 4 a.m. and I never once resented it because she could have been a champion, the best. She could have had what I never could and most people never could. Do you know how rare that chance is? I never got it, but she had it in her grasp.

Emilie was born for the water. But she hasn't been in the pool for two years.

You should have seen her glide through the water: so sleek, such precision on every stroke. Her rotation was impeccable. Her hand would enter the water at the most beautiful angle, with barely a ripple, carve through it. Her posture was perfect, the tightness of her form and the flick of her feet.

The swimming squad scene was cliquey. Emilie is quite shy so didn't really get involved, she just hung out with a couple of friends. I know that all the parents were secretly comparing and competing, two-faced. There was lots of chat about whose kid was favoured by the coach and I was pretty caught up in that. They'd all be nice to your face but I knew what they really thought of us. The competition poolside was fiercer than in the water.

Other kids had private coaches and swim camp but Emilie wasn't born with a silver spoon in her mouth. It was just me and Em against them all. She was just talent, a stand-out. Everyone used to say it would be Emilie who made it. I wanted her to be untouchable, like, no-questions-asked perfect. I wanted everyone to have zero doubts. I guess I was pretty invested.

Emilie's mum says it started to go downhill when she was 13 and a half. She was putting on a bit of weight and I felt she was getting lazy in the pool. No one else seemed to be worried but I needed to push her harder to keep her motivated. I was the one who cared enough to make sure she was flawless. I gave her a straight talk about the fact she was slipping and that she should be thinking about that gold around her neck obsessively. I told her coach to stay on her too, to be ceaseless.

At first, she listened and worked hard. But she didn't make the step-change I needed to see. I kept criticising and pushing so she could see where the next improvement would come from. I'd tell her she wasn't good enough yet, that if she was going to make it, she had to be ready to swim in senior competitions against the best in the world by the age of 14.

I think I got pretty obsessive. It may sound harsh but she couldn't afford to slack off. She had to stick to the time frames. I was doing this for her!

But it didn't work. Her times started to drop. She looked flat in the pool, no energy. One day in the car when I was coaching her she said I was 'damaging her self-esteem' and that she felt like a robot! Some nonsense from one of those busybody parents, no doubt. I told her I was the one she could trust, not them. I would never let her fail.

It all came undone when Emilie had just turned 15, during the regionals. By the day of the competition, I had become pretty frustrated. She hadn't been trying hard enough. She wasn't showing me the killer instinct you need to get ahead.

There was another girl competing from a different district who was on unbelievable form. She was making it look easy. I watched her heats and got agitated as hell. I wanted Emilie to fire up. I could feel all this irritation buzzing in me. In the bay, pre-race, I told her that everyone in the club was watching her. I said if she didn't swim perfectly and finally prove her talent, I would be disappointed and ashamed of her. I don't even know where that came from, it just leapt out of my mouth. I could never be ashamed of her.

She totally lost it and started screaming at me. I was embarrassed that she was freaking out, and I told

her to calm down and smarten up before she got a
slap. That leapt out of my mouth too. Father of the
year. I would never have slapped her, but just me
saying it made her even more wild.

   She said she hated me and if I wanted it so much,
I should get in the pool myself. She said she didn't
want to be perfect. Said she didn't want a gold medal,
she wanted a life and she wanted to eat pizza! Pizza!
Honestly, how could you give up gold for pizza?

   All the other parents heard. I bet they were
sniggering and loving it. I was furious. I shouted at
her, but she would not get in the pool. She picked up
her stuff, changed and left with a friend's mum. That
was the last time she swam. My girl. What a com-
plete failure of a coach and dad I am. And what a
waste.

You can see how Jacques was projecting his perfectionism
onto Emilie. His ceaseless criticism of her eventually dried out
her self-esteem and led to them becoming virtually estranged.
But it was his fear of her failure that fuelled his obsession, so
really it was nothing to do with her. In fact, her reaction,
wanting to withdraw, was a smart survival technique.

   I spoke to Emilie at the same time I spoke to Jacques, a
couple of years later. She told me she felt her dad could not see
or hear her. That she felt used and angry. 'The whole "amazing daughter" thing was just a big lie. He just saw me as a
swimmer who could get him a medal,' she said.

   Jacques didn't know how to reconcile with Emilie, which
he desperately wanted, because he couldn't truly see what had
happened. He thought the problems were his harshness and his

failure as a coach. But this is a level above the real reason: that once his fear of failure took him over, he stopped relating to Emilie, and couldn't see her as anything other than a project to be perfected.

Jacques needed to look deeper, to see, face and replace his fear before he could hope to reconnect with her. That's why he hadn't managed to reconcile in the two years after Emilie stopped swimming. Without him having insight into what really happened, any apology would be half-baked. These are the main points of our conversation:

Pippa: 'Where are you at now, Jacques?'

Jacques: 'I feel sad. I miss my girl a lot.'

Pippa: 'I bet.'

Jacques: 'She is the brightest star in the sky, you know.'

Pippa: 'Are you a star in that sky too?'

Jacques: 'Me? I'm not a star. (Huffs) I am definitely not a star in anyone's sky. (Long, agitated silence) More like a dungeon-dweller.'

Pippa: 'What can you tell me about dungeon-dwellers? Why do they dwell there?'

Jacques: (Huffs, shifting uncomfortably in his chair, angry tone) 'Because it is unlit.'

Pippa: 'They don't want to be seen?'

Jacques: 'No. (Long pause) No, I suppose they don't.'

Pippa: 'What's it like down in the dungeon?'

Jacques: 'I hate it — I hate this conversation. (Pause as he resisted my question, struggled to go there in his imagination) The walls are slimy and cold. It is damp and narrow, it stinks of decay. You can't breathe well.'

Pippa:	'Who else is there?'
Jacques:	'Every loser is there.'
Pippa:	'OK. It sounds scary to me.'
Jacques:	'It is not a pleasant place to spend your days, no.'
Pippa:	'That's why you had to make sure Emilie doesn't dwell there?'
Jacques:	(Shocked, stares for a long time and then puts his head in his hands and openly moans out loud) 'Oh my God.'
Pippa:	'She doesn't belong there?'
Jacques:	'All this time I've been keeping her away from being a loser like me.'
Pippa:	'What would happen if Emilie lost?'
Jacques:	(Longest pause) 'She is no dungeon-dweller. That girl will be a star whatever she does. She is amazing. She lights me up whatever she does.'
Pippa:	'I wonder where you two might find a middle ground to hang out between the skies and the dungeons?'
Jacques:	'That's what I need to find! A good open meeting spot where we can see each other.'
Pippa:	'Sounds like a plan . . .'

Notice that the emphasis is not on what was right or wrong, or on diagnosing or fixing what happened for Jacques and Emilie. When we jump from descriptions to prescriptions, we lose the more soulful and change-making meanings of our behaviour.

The image he saw for his fear was him as the loser in the unlit dungeon. And his image of a meeting place easily stuck with him, too. It was middle ground, a psychologically open space between him and his daughter, a place where they could re-story their relationship. He would have to come out of his 'cave' to meet her here, as her dad, not as an agitated and fearful dungeon-dwelling loser. Without the image, we might never have known that was where his self-esteem called home.

Like the imaginary dungeon, perfectionism was a place for Jacques to hide. If he could just make Emilie unbeatable, if he could prove her to be perfect, the world would be 'safe' for her, and maybe a bit safer for him too.

Like Caroline in the previous chapter, Jacques was operating in a high-fear environment. He described it as being more competitive at the side of the pool than in the pool. As a child, he had taken in the message that he was a loser, which had made him over-controlling and perfectionistic with himself. Then the environment at the edge of the pool triggered him to tighten his grip even more, but this time focused on Emilie.

In Jacques' case, his perfectionism was projected on to his daughter, but more often it results in people having these un-attainably high standards for themselves. How can you tell if it's perfectionism rather than simply high standards? The answer is in how it feels. Can you recognise you have a need, like Jacques, to avoid being, or being seen as, a failure? The other clue that what you're living is damaging perfectionism is that when you miss a target you set for yourself (or someone else does), then you feel the need to up your levels of control and self-criticism.

CHAPTER 12

Distorted fear: self-criticism

Everybody judges. You do, I do, and we get judged too. We judge people and situations all day, every day. He's good, but she's bad; they are like us, but those guys are outsiders; she's an ally but he's a threat; this is right so that is wrong; this is a good deal and that's a rip-off.

We do it because our minds are chock-full and it's a relief to simplify our environments into black and white. Judgement, on its own, is not a problem. In fact, it's the opposite: it's a life skill that helps you make decisions and draw conclusions. To judge is to form an opinion based on thoughts, feelings and evidence.

So how does a habit as common as judgement turn harmful?

Sometimes we judge with positive intentions, but often they are negative. When fear is behind our judgements, we judge not out of a desire to simplify our mental traffic but to deal with a perceived threat.

One source of fear is our many and various unconscious biases. These learned stereotypes are deeply ingrained, which makes them very powerful. The scariest – and most prevalent – are those we all hold around race, sex, power and privilege structures and religion.

For example, if you're a man, you might unthinkingly hold a door open for a woman to walk through before you, yet you wouldn't for another man. The woman is likely to be capable of holding the door for herself but the bias you've absorbed is that part of your responsibility as a man is to protect women.

Holding the door is not the problem. But while your action might be courteous and friendly, underneath there may be an unexamined bias about the difference in roles and capabilities of men and women.

Having these biases can make us more likely to judge other people negatively. This can lead to tribalism (people like me are best, people unlike me are less than) and the scarcity mindset (there isn't enough to go around, so get yours first and keep hold of it).

Playing on our unconscious biases and fears is the bread and butter of both political and marketing campaigns. For example, you may remember the billboard van scheme piloted by Theresa May in 2013 when she was Home Secretary. Vans painted with the message 'Go home or face arrest' drove around six London boroughs. The stated aim was to create a 'hostile environment' that would make illegal immigrants hand themselves in, but you could see it as the Conservatives tapping into voters fear and making immigrants into the enemy, the other.

In order to judge 'cleanly', that is without undue fear, you need to look at your own biases and the fears that sit under them.

Negative judgement (criticism) of others is a form of power-play. Add in self-interested, hyper-individual cultures or organisations – particularly where the person at the top believes in dog-eat-dog – and criticism becomes a contact sport. The critic temporarily gets the high ground, feels clever, important and in power. And the judged find themselves bewildered or looking for cover.

There's another type of criticism, which can be the most aggressive, mean and debilitating kind as it comes straight from the voice in your own head. There is no other voice that damages your potential and ambition as much as that of self-criticism. No one finds fault with you, belittles and diminishes you quite like you do.

You may even spill out your self-criticism for others to hear. I have a fines system in place with my mum: £1 for every self-deprecating comment she makes (and I make her pay it). She occasionally gets a pound back from me too.

Other people keep up a hidden internal dialogue of unfiltered negativity, all of which is about not being good enough, or of not being lovable in some way – I'm too stupid, too fat, too thin, too ugly, too poor, too inexperienced, too different, too uncoordinated, too useless . . .

In the five stories below, you'll see in two of them, the judgement comes from outside then the person starts to believe them and internalises it, turning the emotion inwards. And in the other three, a situation triggers existing inner judgements.

When funny isn't so funny

'It's just banter, lad. Don't get all precious about it, princess.'

This was the kind of interaction Mo often had with his new coach. He felt he should be able to take it when he was ridiculed and, at first, he did.

But when the 'banter' took on a racist undertone, he really started to struggle. His coach made comments such as, 'Smile, mate, if we can't see your teeth we can't see whether whether you're offside at night.' And, 'Even though you've had a good week on the track, I'm not playing you at wing back this game, mate. But don't be getting your Gs from the hood on me.'

At first, Mo let the fact he was angry and upset show. But he felt it made the banter worse, more edgy, more intense. And because all the comments were done with the light-hearted tone of banter, it made it hard to be able to get enough of a handle on them to respond to them. When he was asked to pick up the cones or stay back and collect the bibs, he felt targeted. It was subtle, but he instinctively knew that if he complained, he would get more.

The coach's comments began to spoil Mo's focus on his training. He was on tenterhooks, constantly waiting for the next comment. With each one, he tried to deflect attention and laugh it off, but his heart sank deeper.

Worse, he felt isolated and lonely. He couldn't understand why no other player, black or white, on the squad spoke up on his behalf. Was it OK with everyone else? He found himself unable to open up or form friendships on the team. Mo even felt too ashamed to tell his family. He knew his mum would go straight to the coach and give him a piece of her mind, but he was afraid what would happen next, that he'd never live it down in the team, or never be selected again.

Mo's feelings needed somewhere to go and, over the season, they eventually turned inwards, turning into self-criticism and deflating his self-esteem. As the casual abuse became worse, he felt like the proverbial 'boiling frog', stuck in the pot and being slowly cooked to death. 'They hate you, just quit,' his inner critic said. 'You're so pathetic. You should stand up for yourself but you're a loser, not man enough.' His teammates kept an uneasy distance from him, probably to avoid being included in the 'banter'.

Once, around this time, he did push back on the coach. It was when a Drake tune was playing on the team bus. 'Your bro on the mic, home boy!' his coach said.

'Coach, why do you keep talking about me being black – you jealous?' he said, with a fake laugh.

His coach looked him straight in the eye and replied: 'Don't be playing the racist card, lad, it's just bonding. This is what footy is all about. Just keep your Afro on.'

'You will never belong, loser,' Mo's inner critic told him.

At the time we spoke, Mo felt trapped, as if he had a constant weight on him that he could not

budge or go around. He had sunk into negative
feeling and self-doubt. The conversation that helped
him see the fear that sat beneath his self-criticism
went something like this:

Pippa:	'This has been a tough time for you,'
Mo:	'Hmm. I don't know where to start.'
Pippa:	'Maybe start by trying to describe how you've been feeling. What's it been like?'
Mo:	'Really drained. I've been feeling exhausted.'
Pippa:	'How so?'
Mo:	'It's like I'm waiting for what's next, always on guard.'
Pippa:	'Yes. Say some more?'
Mo:	'It sounds weird but I almost feel like I've been stalked or something. Like this feeling that it's going to happen again any minute is following me around and stalking me.'
Pippa:	'Yes, that does sound tiring. What is the stalker like?'
Mo:	(Pause) 'You know when you get a really long shadow at the end of the day? Sort of like that. With long bony fingers that can give me a little jab in the ribs any time and big long feet that can trip me up.'
Pippa:	'What would happen if you tripped?'
Mo:	'Well, erm, I'd look stupid. (Pause) I'd look like an idiot, wouldn't I? I already look like an idiot.'
Pippa:	'This stalker that's following you around. What do you think he wants from you?'
Mo:	(Pause) 'Maybe he wants to see if I'm good enough.'

Pippa: 'Good enough at what?'

Mo: (Long pause) 'Well, I'm good enough at footy, it's
         not that. Not being big-headed but I know that
         even if this chance fell through I'd be OK. It's just,
         you know, what if I'm not good at standing up and
         being counted? At being a man?'

Pippa: 'It's the fear of not being a good enough man that's
         stalking you?'

Mo: 'Yeah. Yeah, I think that's it. The racism
         annoys the hell out of me and it's obviously not
         right. But it's the fact I haven't been able to stand
         up to it that's getting me down. I'm worried
         I'm spineless.'

Pippa: 'I suspect many people find that it's not so easy too.
         Who in you might be capable, do you think?'

Mo: (Pause) 'In my first few weeks at school, there was
         a year twelve kid bullying a weedy year seven in
         the dinner queue. The little kid was suffering.
         Even though I was a year seven too, I went and
         shoved the bully, got in his face, told him to stop
         being an idiot and to grow up. Everyone laughed
         so he was embarrassed and he stopped hassling the
         kid. The kid didn't thank me, he just got out of
         there but that didn't matter. I felt like I'd shone a
         light on the bigger kid's unfair behaviour and it
         made him stop. I felt good.'

Pippa: 'Sounds like you could do with that light-shiner at
         the moment?'

Mo: 'Totally. This needs a bit of light shining on it,
         doesn't it? I think it does.'

Pippa: 'OK. Who in you can do that?'

Mo: 'The dinner-queue kid can.'
Pippa: 'And then the shadow following you around won't
           be so big perhaps . . .'
Mo: 'Totally. Shadows can't survive in the light.'

You can see how Mo's fear of not being a good enough man was replaced with the idea of himself as a 'light-shiner', someone who'd uncover the dark and hidden and buried culture of racism.

Mo acted. One day, after a training session, he gathered his courage and approached the coach. Mo told the coach that if he made a racist remark during a game or training session, Mo would come to him in private afterwards, strike a match and look him in the eye until it burned out, to remind him that racism burned.

And he did it. The first time, the coach howled with laughter and eyeballed him back. The second time, the coach was uncomfortable and tried to walk away. The third time, he apologised. Mo didn't need to strike a match again.

'I ended up second-guessing everything'

Harjeet was hired into a large commercial real estate agency from another industry as an experienced leader who could create change. She had a track record of not being afraid to rattle cages, and as someone who got results.

When she accepted the role, she wasn't sure about the lack of cultural diversity in the organisation or its openness, but the opportunity to work with a high-profile brand was too good to miss. As she began to reach and beat her targets, there were approving nods. But when she started to be noticed by important people, she was swiftly reined in with covert criticism and judgement by the old guard. These were the messages she heard:

> 'This is a place where you need to earn your stripes.'
>
> 'There are people who have been around a lot longer than you who don't choose to say so much.'
>
> 'You're an outsider so I can't expect you to understand how this industry works.'
>
> 'I know they think your work is competent, but frankly they're no experts. You're a long way off.'
>
> 'This looks like you're profile-seeking. It's better if someone with more experience does it.'
>
> 'The results were well underway when you walked in the door.'
>
> 'You should understand how much we value "humility", Harjeet. In my view, that means waiting until someone asks you for your opinions.'
>
> 'People last in this place for a reason. Read the play. Work out who is who.'

'It didn't take a lot to work out the underlying meaning,' she said. 'Back off and back down.'

The judgements made her second-guess herself. It became difficult for her to feel safe to lead and operate, and to get her job done. When she entered a room, she would notice the old guard whispering, dropping their eyes.

Her levels of fear ramped up. 'In order to feel safe, I became hyper-vigilant about what I said. I know I said less, too. Along with feeling confused, I also started to feel resentment and paranoia. The place was something else. I felt so constrained and powerless. I don't know if it was me but I'd never experienced this before. I felt as if the only option was to shut up.

'I started to second-guess my colleagues. I'd think: maybe they all feel this way about me? Do they all hate me? I'm too different. Maybe I'm not really up to the job after all. Maybe I should move on.'

When Harjeet began to describe her fear of being criticised, her images were of feeling hunted.

'I'm little. I'm prey. I'm a small weak animal hiding in large reeds and tall grasses. I'm trying to navigate through them but I'm lost and I have no idea where I'm going or why. There are large footprints where the predators have been and I know they are still lurking around me, watching and waiting to pounce. I know I have to move forward because it's not safe here but I want to dig down and bury myself. I want to be somewhere else.'

Once Harjeet could see and understand how her fear was at work, she could start to look at what might be more useful moving forward.

Harjeet replaced her fear of being judged with an internal story about herself as a visiting 'educator', who was showing the old guard how their predatory language and behaviour was getting in the way of performance. It took a lot of courage and self-compassion to act on this, but this sense of purpose felt life-changing for her, and infused her with confidence.

She targeted a couple of the main perpetrators and had one-on-one conversations with them. Despite being anxious, she tried to be as open and real and warm as she could. She steeled herself to maintain eye contact and speak with composure, telling each guy that when she heard their comments, she felt unwelcome. And that was starting to make her want to leave or withdraw, and was affecting her performance. But she wanted to do well for them and the company.

People were certainly taken aback at her honesty. But because Harjeet was direct and handled these discussions discreetly, so lowering the threat, some of them took it on board. One person responded that he had never thought about it like that. Another said that he felt he was helping by toughening her up for the culture, but now he realised that his words weren't having the intended effect.

The courageous conversations helped educate Harjeet's colleagues and make their behaviour much more conscious. But it also positioned her as no walk-over. This was powerful because she could see herself carrying the will to speak up, warmly and with compassion for herself and others, forward through her career.

'I felt as if my stupidity was tattooed across my head'

'If you keep your mouth shut, no one will know you are stupid.' This was the line John absorbed during his childhood: from the school playground, the family dinner table and playing football with his mates. It wasn't necessarily directed at him, at least most of the time, but it became a favourite phrase of his own inner voice.

John spent most of his school years desperately trying to avoid having to speak at the front of the class, his worst fear, because he thought he would definitely mess it up and everyone would know he was an idiot. He hovered at the back of the classroom with his inner critic playing in his head as if it was on a loudspeaker.

He grew up to be a deeply humble, intelligent and inquisitive man, a talented independent craftsman who was full of ideas. He had a lot to say that was valuable, but his inner critic kept him shrunk back and anxious, preferring to look and act less capable than he was so he didn't risk saying something 'stupid'.

When someone was introduced to him by their job title, his inner critic would say: 'You've nothing to say to a person like this. They are so much more important than you.'

He'd worked on his own most of his adult life but, in his mid-thirties, an opportunity arose to join a local collective of progressive artists. His wife and family encouraged him to do it. They felt it would bring the recognition he deserved. The idea of recognition was, of course, terrifying to John.

Eventually, he agreed. He turned up to the communal workshop with his stomach in knots. On the first morning there was a group gathering, sitting on stools around the big oak table in the workshop, everyone chatting and drinking coffee. John felt as if his own inferiority was tattooed across his forehead in black ink. He felt stiff with quiet dread, hands clasped around his coffee cup, hoping not to be noticed.

One of the other artists was a sculptor who'd studied in London and worked in Italy. He leant over the table and said to John, 'I really love your work, John, it has such a raw and real texture.'

John's inner critic immediately translated this into 'badly finished and colloquial'. 'Oh, it's pretty average,' John spluttered, shrugging and smiling. The message from his inner critic was: 'Don't speak, you sound stupid. You are a total fraud, self-taught and basic, and you know nothing about this world.'

When John started to explore how his fear felt, he came up with an image of a desert-like landscape, parched and unrelenting with no shade. He described being dry-mouthed and husk-like when he was around 'better' people, with anything lush and nourishing buried way inside the sharp and prickly cactus-like exterior that was there to protect him from being 'seen'.

It took a long time for John to face and let go of his fear. Because self-criticism was so entrenched in him, it took a while for him to work out what it had cost. Initially he thought it had only had consequences for him, but he uncovered that it meant he often chose to withdraw rather than to help out, so it was affecting others too. And it was this understanding, that he was acting selfishly, that broke the spell for John. He was able to step forward because he discovered that his desire to be seen as generous was bigger than his desire to hide away.

Now he was motivated to change. He wanted to let go of the story of himself as stupid and not worth listening to. Rather than withholding the nourishment of ideas he had to share, he moved towards his values of generosity. He changed his images to people drinking at an 'oasis' of ideas. This meant he could start to see his contributions to the group, his ideas and thoughts, as a way to help other people rather than keeping them to (or for) himself.

If your self-critic is loud and dominating, ask yourself whether it gets in the way of who you'd like to be for others. Ask what your voice and message could offer to the world beyond you. Does it contain something you value deeply, like John valuing generosity? Even if you don't think enough of yourself to push back at the critic at first, over time that value will encourage you to do so.

Self-criticism is exhausting. Remember to be gentle with yourself, praise yourself for your progress day by day, and try to deal only in facts, not opinions.

'Nobody must see my ugly, disgusting body'

During a sexy conversation, Mischa, who was 17, sent her boyfriend Joe a Snapchat picture of herself posing naked.

She knew it was risky but she trusted him and it was thrilling in the heat of the moment. Mischa assumed the picture had gone into the black hole of the internet, never to be seen again. But even though Joe had sworn to Mischa that he wouldn't save the image, he had screenshot it.

Showing off, Joe showed the image to his best friend. A bit later, without Joe knowing, his friend picked up Joe's phone and air-dropped the picture to himself. Probably because Joe knew he'd done the wrong thing – twice – his senses were alert so his friend's behaviour made him suspicious. He became angry, challenged his friend and made him delete the shot immediately.

Joe was afraid that his friend had forwarded it or kept it somehow, even though he said he hadn't. And he thought that if Mischa found out what Joe had done, she'd definitely dump him. But his conscience wouldn't let him drop it, so he decided that he'd tell her.

Mischa was both devastated and hurt. She was scared the picture might surface and be shared. But the worst of it, she said, her face burning up, wasn't that people would see their sexy exchange or even that he kept the shot, it was that people would see her 'ugly, disgusting body'.

Joe was relieved Mischa didn't seem to be that focused on his decisions to save and share the shot. And he couldn't believe that what she was most worried about was people seeing her body. 'Babe, you're gorgeous,' he said. 'That's the least of any worries.' He was bewildered that she'd turned on herself, when it was him who'd done something wrong.

The picture didn't surface. But Joe's friend had told other friends that it existed. When a couple of them asked Mischa, as a joke, if she'd send them a Snapchat too, Mischa's fear immediately turned inwards to violent self-criticism and shame. Her inner voice said, 'What the hell were you thinking, you slut? You're an idiot. You might as well have put it online yourself and shown everyone your saggy boobs and scaly skin and repulsive cellulite. Joe is just using you, but that's the only way you could have anyone. You are never going to be taken seriously now.'

When Mischa began to talk about and find an image for her fear and shame, she said: 'It's like this feeling came out physically on my skin as blushing. My red, burning face showed everyone the inferiority and inadequacy that were on fire inside me. I felt that everyone was looking at my embarrassment and fear, splattered on my skin in red blotches. I wanted to just turn to ashes rather than continue to feel I was burning alive.'

In fact, she said she felt so exposed that she might as well have been naked, despite the fact the picture never surfaced and the comments only came from a small handful of boys.

Mischa was suffering (burning) despite the fact that the picture wasn't shared beyond Joe and his friend. And she was suffering because her fear had turned vicious and gone inward. She needed to let it out.

Over time Mischa created a new image: with every blush, she was allowing some of her fear and shame to escape and evaporate through her skin. And when that happened, it made more room for self-compassion and love. Eventually, when she blushed, she started to feel grateful for doing so. She also looked for a 'shame mentor' in the world of literature and found Maya Angelou, whose quote 'When you know better, you do better' became Mischa's mantra.

'I didn't feel like a real mother'

Seren couldn't seem to breastfeed her newborn baby, James. She asked for help from her midwife, then from her mum, then from her friends who had more experience. The message she got from all of them was 'keep trying'.

Seren had desperately wanted this baby, had tried for a long time before conceiving. Throughout her pregnancy, she felt an intense pressure to get everything right, to be 'excellent' at every part of the journey.

She read every book, went to every class, and drank every green juice. She continued to run until very late pregnancy, not reducing the demands on herself or her body. Later, she admitted that she got more controlling as the birth approached. For the birth itself, she had a detailed plan in her mind of how it would all go.

The birth didn't follow the plan, and ended up as an emergency C-section. While James was born healthy, she felt she hadn't given birth 'properly'. And so she'd failed this natural 'rite of passage' to real womanhood. But she tucked away her sense of failure from everyone's view and tried to focus on the baby now in her arms.

Seren knew from her research that new mums often felt overwhelmed, but she was bowled over by the intensity of the demands and how fatigued and emotional she felt. She saw herself as a capable and successful woman but this was tougher than she thought and was going to need even more management and control, she decided.

Not being able to get James to feed – what she considered the absolute basic for looking after a baby – made her feel she was not even beginning to be up to standard. She judged herself as failing at the most important job of her life.

Seren's midwife was dogmatic about breastfeeding: she said any other kind of food was a weak substitute for breast milk and would disadvantage her child's development. These words were rocket fuel for Seren's inner critic. The fear started to rise: she wasn't good enough. Even her baby wasn't going to be good enough.

Seren felt ashamed, too. She thought: 'There is something wrong with you if you can't even do this simple basic human task that every mum can do, like you couldn't even give birth properly. Just get it right! If you can't, you're not a proper mother.'

Her son was simply not getting enough food and continued to cry. Seren blamed herself for not being able to feed or soothe him. She started to dread each feed, to become angry with her own body and deeply self-critical. She couldn't allow herself to accept that sometimes breastfeeding just doesn't work for real, organic reasons.

Finally, after a few weeks and James losing weight, the midwife intervened. She found he couldn't suckle properly as he had a small tied lip and a tied tongue.

When Seren started to explore her fear and shame around breastfeeding, the image she had was of wading through a swampy marsh, hot and humid, trying to swat away mosquitos that were biting her face and chest and scalp. She wanted cool shelter where she could compose herself, but she couldn't get to it because she was bogged down. She needed to slow down and take different steps in order to get unstuck.

Seren was able to replace her fear of not being a good enough mum with a new idea of herself as someone who did have the ability to wade through even a swamp when needed. In fact, she could get through anything, she knew how to suffer and push through. She was strong at it; she said she had her waders at the ready when most would sink!

Recognising how controlling she had become, she also decided to be what she called a 'beauty-hunter', which she described as a deliberate will to see and find beauty in her own and her baby's life.

This mission helped Seren to let go and reinterpret herself as a good enough mother, with much broader criteria. She started to deliberately plan for beauty in her surroundings, her conversations, in the language she used, in her home and in her heart. The beauty she hunted could be anything from stepping outside at sunset, looking at the moon and stopping to listen to birdsong to bringing colour and texture into her house. She was reimagining the story of what made a good day and a good mother, and it was a great help in quietening her inner critic.

None of these five people had done anything to deserve the damaging judgements and self-criticism they experienced. But they each got stuck in the cement of their own critical minds until they could deliberately shift their perspectives. Images helped them to do this.

What strikes me about all these stories is how much each person lost to their criticism and to the fears that came up when they felt judged. They lost time, confidence, opportunity, dignity, well-being and presence as well as massive amounts of mental energy.

Do any of these scenarios feel familiar to you? Do you find yourself judging others or yourself in damaging ways? Maybe you have allowed other people's judgements to knock you off course? Criticism sticks like Velcro; even when we know rationally that it's not true, it's hard to see past this surface level. But whether your judgements are about you or others, they are a misguided strategy for handling your fear of inadequacy. That's why the people in the stories found it so valuable to broaden the way they saw their fear taking over their self-stories.

You can also see, in this approach, how powerful it was for them to use images to describe what was going on for them, what was sitting under their judgement. Reread the See and Face sections in chapter 8 to help you start thinking about what might lie underneath your judgement, of yourself or others.

What do the stories say to you?

I hope that these stories have helped you begin to see your own fears. It's often only when people are in real pain or at rock bottom – like Jacques becoming estranged from his daughter, Caroline losing her job, or Jake getting into bar fights – that they start this. But if you can accept that when fear pops up, it's worth tackling straight away, you'll cause yourself a lot less suffering.

Facing your fears, seeing how they are affecting you and other people, is not easy. But it isn't nearly as hard as covering up, glossing over and pretending. Because, as you can see, living like that is chronically draining.

It requires a particular kind of courage, the courage to be vulnerable, to say, 'I think I'm repeating the same mistake' or 'I think I'm avoiding this opportunity because what I feel underneath is fear'. Men especially – but anyone over-conditioned into being tough – may find they have a blind spot around seeing their fear, because culturally it has been associated with weakness. But in fact it's way more courageous and harder emotionally to see and face your fear than to push through and ignore it.

The next chapter is about the ups and downs of what you might experience, as you grow and change and face your fears.

CHAPTER 13

Getting into the mess

When people go through the process of facing their fears, like the stories you've just read, it's hard to convey the extent of their struggle. But struggle and mess deserve as much of a place in our hearts and conversations as accomplishment and success. They're a valid, meaningful part of your life, not something to cover up.

By now, you'll have started to see how fear is coming both from outside and inside you and you may have an idea of what your fears might look like too. But it may feel a bit messy at times. That's because it's part of life: and, after all, life is light and dark, good and bad, struggle and glory, pain and joy. Nobody has it all sorted. And we shouldn't aim for that anyway, as it's a false ideal.

Human beings improve and thrive because we are adaptable. We can change, even our brains can change. And we can fully participate in that – nudge along our own change. That's amazing.

So, why don't we do it more? Why do we get stuck in the same ruts and patterns? Because we don't always want to look at who we are, personally or culturally. And maybe we don't want to get into the mess.

But if you want to live wholeheartedly, to win at life in more deeply satisfying ways, you do need to 'find out' about yourself. Assuming that things won't ever change will leave you doing the same exhausting dance with *not-good-enough* fears all your life. And if you look for quick hacks and top tips, you will likely be disappointed. Change is a long game, not a pitch and putt.

When we are struggling, we can get stuck in the weeds of comparing ourselves to people who look as if they have it all together. Comparison makes you more likely to notice other people's success stories than their failures. But pretty much all of us encounter bumps in the road and struggle in some way, sometimes.

One of those struggles might be feeling shame. Mo struggled deeply to come to terms with his teammates, because they didn't say anything while he suffered racism and was mocked. Because people looked away, he felt that there really must be something wrong with him. And so his shame deepened. In reality, his teammates probably just didn't know how to get into the mess of talking about something that is hard.

Struggle is natural. A chick hatching out of its shell does it, a mother giving birth does it. Psychologically, it's part of maturing and growing, a fundamental experience.

If we hide it when we struggle or suffer, or brush it away, we miss vital opportunities for healing and fulfilment. Struggle forces us to find solutions. It can mean grinding through the difficulty or stepping back until you see it more clearly.

You're likely to feel like giving up at some point. Caroline was so remorseful and ashamed after losing her job for pushing out her protégé, her first reaction was to want to leave her profession. Harjeet was forging her career in a male-dominated industry, but after her fear was provoked in a hostile company, she was ready to turn her back on it, which would have meant throwing away so much valuable experience.

Both of them kept feeling the pain and going through the struggle. But each one would acknowledge that facing their fears was a way through to knowing themselves better, letting go of the power fear held over them, and to greater fulfilment.

There's another advantage: when you struggle and are open about it, you'll notice all the people who've got your back and who care about you. You might even be surprised by how they step up, as shown by Jake's parents' loving reaction when he told them he was gay. Struggle can be a portal to connecting, if you let it.

In fact, struggling is a necessary part of soul-making, growing and learning from what doesn't go right.

The poet John Keats puts this idea beautifully:[12]

Do you not see how necessary a World of Pains and
troubles is to school an Intelligence and make it a soul?
A Place where the heart must feel and suffer in a
thousand diverse ways!

Soul has dark and light in it. Life does too. It's not real or helpful to expect to be perfectly happy, positive and comfortable all the time, nor is it real to expect all struggle and suffering.

Cleaning out your rubbish

It is tempting to pretend there isn't a dark side to life, or that you can control it. But when you acknowledge how you feel, you can find tremendous freedom and peace. Imagine if people saw your insides instead of your outsides, so all the things you think of as faults and all your greatest fears were exposed. Then where would all that negative energy have to lie in ambush? The answer is: nowhere.

Being in denial, pretending everything is fine when it's not, will only add to the distorted fears and emotional waste that we drag around.

The idea of emotional waste is a useful one. It covers any emotion and resulting behaviour that's redundant or destructive, no longer useful or required – and yet you're still hanging on to it. It is junk emotion, scrap, rubbish.

Unnecessary drama is emotional waste. Bitching, gossiping, worrying, blaming, resenting and hating are all emotional waste. Empty 'shoulds' and 'can'ts' – for example, 'I should feel differently' or 'I can't control it' or 'I won't be able to do it' – are too. All of the above are wasteful because they only give you relief from uncomfortable emotions for a fleeting moment.

Ignoring or repressing your fears also leads to emotional waste. This happens when you'll do anything to not be present in your own life in order to avoid feeling the difficult feelings. You might find yourself with unhelpful neurotic tendencies such as fixating on things way before you need to, obsessing over details or repetitively worrying that you won't be able to cope. You might find that you numb yourself with food or alcohol, distract yourself with shopping, or seek the constant stimulation of gaming.

Like an island of plastic choking the ocean, emotional waste can build up and become problematic if left unprocessed. When you have a build-up, you're likely to become a little toxic to the people around you. It may seem to you that you are keeping your emotions tidied away, but the emotional energy has to go somewhere. Energy exchanges happen between people whether they're planned or not, in your non-verbal behaviour, mood, tone and sharp or even fake-sweet words.

You could compare the breakdown of emotional waste to how compost is made. The process of seeing and facing your *not-good-enough* fears and other emotional waste is like making emotional compost, if you like. Doing this won't be clean or neat, it may even stink. But with both compost and fears, a lack of air makes more stink. The more you open the lid and turn over the compost, the more you keep seeing and tackling your fears, the quicker they will decompose.

The things that might stink could include acknowledging how your fear has limited you (this can be hard to look at). Or recognising that you've brought other people into your fear. Perhaps you have behaved in destructive, confusing ways to a partner by starting fights or sulking, while not being able to explain fully what's wrong. Or think about Jacques: his obsession to make his daughter into a great swimmer grew until he could no longer connect with her at all. The emotional waste from this was destroying their relationship – until he opened the lid.

Making compost is also a good analogy because it takes time to do properly. Similarly, you don't need to try to move through your all your fears to fix them quickly. But most of all, just as compost makes plants grow and flourish, your emotional compost will fuel the green shoots of your new and better practices, behaviours, narratives and beliefs.

PART 4

Replacing *not-good-enough* fear

This final section is to help you think about different ways to replace the fears that are controlling you. You'll find some ideas of how to grow new and useful practices, behaviours and beliefs to replace the old destructive ones.

I've included seven ways of thinking about change. These are the ones that have made the biggest difference in my work. Of course, not every one will feel right to you or be relevant to your situation. But it's worth reading all of them to find those you can work with.

Most of the time we just don't have the patience and tolerance to build different stories for ourselves, to rewrite a more purposeful script. It's always going to feel so much easier to stay in our comfort zone, to do what we've always done. Hopefully these stories will give you inspiration and motivation to start.

As you read about these people, you'll see that none of their stories is perfect or has a pretty conclusion that can be tied up with a little bow. Because, as I've said before, perfect is a rubbish ideal. Also, none of the people involved had crystal-clear, unchanging values and principles, or completely understood their passion or purpose from the start. And neither do you need to.

What you can do as you're reading is simply ask yourself: could I do this?

CHAPTER 14

Replace fear with a different story

What do you tell yourself, about you? Are you 'the smart one', 'the different one', 'the black sheep' or perhaps 'the safe pair of hands'?

Think about the more subtle stories you buy into about what's possible in life – and what's not. A few I've heard are: 'It's just never been done in this family', 'It's not worth trying', 'It's always going to fail', 'It can't be helped', 'This is the way it is in this place', 'It won't happen in our lifetime'.

The stories we tell ourselves have a lot of power. This chapter is about how replacing them can have a far-reaching effect in lessening fear too.

We build our identity and our beliefs about what's possible on the back of stories we take on as true. The stories are about both ourselves and the way things are.

But are these stories real, definitive truths? In fact, George Mpanga, the British spoken-word artist, rapper and poet better known as George the Poet, has got it right when he says: 'Everything you know is a story. An idea that you've accepted, until the day you cross it out and replace it with a better answer.'[13]

Do you need a new story?

George also says on his podcast, 'Telling your own story is the secret to survival.' What he means is: the pen (or the mic, in his case) is in your hands. You control your story, even when you don't control your circumstances.

If you tell yourself that you're a perfectionist or a harsh self-critic or not good enough or too jealous, then that is what will become (or remain) true. But – and this is key – the story only stays true until you cross it out and replace it with a better story, one that makes you stronger and offers more possibilities. You can rewrite your own ideas and versions of who you are and what you have inside of you.

Our stories are filled with old beliefs and ideas that are deeply etched into the rock of our identity. Because we've lived through them, retold them again and again, they've become ingrained, so much so that they feel inevitable. But they are not.

How to rewrite your story

Think about how your own story is built. You'll find it's not as concrete or based in reality as you might assume.

Some of our identity story is given to us, such as race, assigned sex, nationality, family of origin stories, maybe our religious faith. Some of our identity we craft for ourselves, such as our profession, our philosophies, in part our persona, our relationships. And some of our identity just takes hold of us, such as our illnesses, adversity and our emotions, including fear.

We are made up of lots of different stories. Some examples of positive stories might be:

> 'The first woman in the family to go to university.'
> 'The only rap artist to challenge the victim mindset.'
> 'Part of a new generation who don't accept the status quo on climate.'
> 'You have your grandad's spirit even though you never met him. He never gave in.'
> 'You come from a long line of courageous women.'

And some negative examples of stories might be:

> 'Nobody in our family could work in a white-collar job.'
> 'I was rubbish at maths at school, so I can't apply for that job.'
> 'Partners always cheat on me.'
> 'I'm an outsider.'
> 'The men in my family die young because of their lifestyle.'

You'll see how these negative stories are underpinned by fear. The source of these stories is what I called the 'tragedy of low expectations' in chapter 5. And the upshot is, if you live by these stories, they become a self-fulfilling prophecy.

But our identity isn't built like a brick wall, one solid layer cemented on top of the next. Because parts of us are always changing, our identity is always flowing and moving.

In addition, our minds are powerful enough to play an active part in reshaping our identity. The eighteenth-century physician Dr John Haygarth was one of the first people to show the existence of the placebo effect. Dr Haygarth conducted experiments using metal pointers that were, at the time, sold as being able to 'draw out' disease. He compared the effect to fake wooden ones. And he found that both types worked equally well, if people believed they were being treated and healed.

What does this mean for the stories we tell ourselves? Since then, more research has added to the position that the placebo effect demonstrates the intense power of belief to create an experience. The point is that this in turn can create our reality. We are coming to understand that we have likely really underrated the power of this, as Johann Hari points out for depression.

In his book, *Lost Connections: Uncovering the Real Causes of Depression – and the Unexpected Solutions* (2018),[14] Johann writes:

> When you give a patient a medical treatment, you are really giving her two things. You are giving her a drug, which will usually have a chemical effect on her body in some way. And you are giving her a story – about how the treatment will affect her.

What we believe to be true has a powerful effect on the way we perceive and create our reality. It is not the same as 'pretending'. We are always making our reality in some way, through our attitudes, assumptions, beliefs and, most of all, through our narratives.

We can imagine an alternate self and an alternate life. This isn't a one-time thing: we can write a draft, cross bits out, tear it up and write another. Or we can stick with most of the old draft and write one specific new chapter that's needed, for example, on getting past perfectionism or self-judgement.

We can try on new identities and if we like them, plan ways to make them permanent. We do not have to be run by a story that's no longer working for us. That's true of individuals but also of places and organisations, too.

Those toxic or stale organisations and teams we discussed in Part 1 don't have to be run by a defunct story either. You'll need the courage to see and acknowledge the institutionalised fear, maybe the fear of being judged, being irrelevant, excluded or rejected and of course of not being good enough.

What story goes with the feeling you have when you walk into the place? It could be 'this will never change while the CEO is still here' or 'this is just how entrepreneurs are'.

What images go with that feeling? Maybe it's like being on a rollercoaster, hanging on with white knuckles, too much air rushing past for you to do anything but scream?

If you face the fear in your organisation or team, what is the true cost of that fear-based narrative? Your well-being? Your curiosity? Your authenticity? Your better performance? Now you have Seen and Faced the fear, what story do you want to write to Replace it?

A new social enterprise initiative called AMIN NIMA, by a Ghanaian former footballer, King Osei Gyan, is a great example of flipping the script on an old story. King is from an area in the capital Accra known as Nima. The name comes from the Hausa language in the Islamic religion and means 'blessing town'. But Nima has a difficult history.

To the untrained eye, Nima is a rundown shanty town. It has poor housing, sanitation and drainage, poor infrastructure and services. Opportunities for education are limited and unemployment is high. The people of Nima are known to be hardy, but crime and poor health are a reality. In places, the streets are a metre high with garbage and waste on which cows and goats and chickens hang out.

From the outside, the superficial story of Nima is that it's a lost cause, a slum, a 'scary ghetto' with an inevitability of poverty and no opportunity. And that the best thing to do is to get out of there. The assumptions and beliefs have been that Nima people are lacking talent and motivation, and are maybe a little shady. But King – and other young entrepreneurs – are reimagining Nima. With the local community, they are deliberately rewriting the narrative about who and what they are.[15] He says:

> I grew up in a place where people must depend on miracles, and this makes me determined to change this paradigm in my community. By strengthening and building systems that allow people to realise their dreams and not be held back by realities. People need opportunities if they have a talent and the will to work hard. No matter where they are born and grow up. We have to take charge, responsibility and control in what happens in our lives.
>
> We actually came up with the name AMIN by spelling NIMA backwards. This was our first action of changing the perceptions of the community, to start looking at things differently. AMIN, like Amen, is about faith and determination. And you can say AM IN charge, for example. I have power. The name itself is symbolic of the new perspective.
>
> Then we started to look a little deeper and not just accept the surface view. I see a richly diverse and vibrant community of locals and migrants. There are

people of various races, castes and religions who live and work side-by-side in common humanity. This kind of harmony isn't even found in some of the richest areas of the world. I see incredible artists and bold, practical entrepreneurs who can create solutions right in Nima, in Africa, without being dependent on charity and aid. They don't need labels like 'third world' that limit them and condescend to them. I see people with real resilience and spirit. People who understand that riches do not just come in folded paper notes. That wealth comes in the richness of community, talent and what you already have right there.

We're challenging the old story that keeps people down. To do this, we're showcasing talent in the community, using art, music, sport and fashion. We started a division two football club called Nima Kings FC. AminNima music is working with two musicians on live performances and recording, AminNima gallery is planning an exhibition for local artists and AminNima fashion is working on a clothing line that will redefine street fashion.

His guiding slogan for this is 'stubborn on purpose' because he knows that it will take a lot of relentless energy to get there. One Instagram post says: 'Don't mistake my stubbornness for disrespect, my confidence for arrogance or my vagabonding for homelessness.'

It's not that the people of Nima don't need better infrastructure. This isn't accepting how it is and ignoring it or feeling stuck. It's seeing through how it looks on the surface to a new story of possibility and pride.

King and his colleagues are breaking the patterns of inevitability and apathy about what is and what is not possible in this community by changing the narrative, inside Nima and to the outside world.

King is determined to change the way the world sees Nima by demonstrating the everyday brilliance, talent and the humanity in this community on the edge of a bustling city. As he says, 'AMIN NIMA is a state of mind. What do you see, poverty or power? We see Powerty!'

Even when it's not easy to change our circumstances, we can become the architect of our own mindsets, and that impacts our futures, especially the place of fear in them. We can re-story, reimagine, reinterpret our narratives in ways that diminish fear and promote more hope, more strength.

Don't let fear write the story you're in.

Changing the story

'I've been through all of this before,' he says to his heart. "Yes, you have been through all of this before, replies his heart, but you have never been beyond it." '

– Paulo Coelho from Warrior
of the Light: A Manual

Maybe you feel like you've tried to change your story, and you can't?

Once we settle for a story, we are extremely reluctant to shift it. Changing it takes a lot of will and effort because our egos get very attached to our stories.

Asking yourself some of the following questions might help. Try to suspend your cynicism; the answers can be powerful.

And while you're not asking these questions, you may be wasting thousands of hours recycling and replaying fear unnecessarily.

> *Who am I when I am fearful?*
> *How do I act when I am fearful?*
> *What can I do with my time and my talent that's not connected to my old fears?*
> *What do I want my potential to be (not what you see it as now)?*
> *What do I want to contribute to the world that fear holds me back from?*
> *What small or large changes can I make in my environment and the way I show myself to other people that could break the limiting routines I'm in?*

For example, there's one small change I've made recently. I noticed that when I'm working in a male-dominated environment where there's fear in the culture, I dress more plainly and conservatively. Looking back, I can see I do this to make sure I don't draw attention to myself as a woman.

I didn't notice this pattern until I started working somewhere that was much more open to women and the feminine, where I felt freer and more certain that I would be taken on merit. I realised the story I'd been telling myself was this: it wasn't yet 100 percent accepted that a woman would have the roles I have, so I needed to lessen differences. I needed to over-adapt to fit in, to overcome my fear of not being taken seriously as a woman, and of being objectified in some way.

Seeing this pattern, I can now be deliberate in my response to the fear. So next time I'm in a male-dominated environment, I can give myself the permission to just show up as 'me' and not try to be 'them'.

If you already know the beliefs or behaviours that aren't working for you, the story behind them that you don't want any more, that's great.

For example, say your job is making you unhappy. Paul from chapter 1 might have realised, earlier in his career, that being a champion footballer at that team was making him feel anxious and stressed most of the time. There are so many ways he could have changed his story, which doesn't mean he needed to change his circumstances. The story you tell changes the experience you have, even when you're still in difficult circumstances.

He could have started to think of himself as the player who got over injury. Or, going back to the story he told himself when he had the trophy in his hand, change his disappointment to resilience and overcoming adversity. Or he could have seen himself as metamorphosing from a lanky kid to a super-strong man who could tolerate the suffering and still win. Or even see himself as a storyteller for the other injured guys, encouraging and coaching the younger ones. Or he could have seen himself as much loved by his mates – realising that he'd turned away from them but also that he didn't need to, because it was the coach who was an idiot. All of these are possible, and more powerful, stories.

You start the re-story process by changing your perspective on what is already there. Then you can adapt and evolve your story by asking yourself: who can I become?

CHAPTER 15

Replace fear with purpose

A sense of purpose is perhaps the best stabiliser during life's unpredictable ride. So you can use your purpose to help overcome fear.

One way of describing purpose is that it's your contribution to the world beyond you. Another is that it's your central motivation, a driving force and a call to action. Purpose directs your attention, influences your decisions and creates meaning for you.

If a personal goal is about you and your achievements, a purpose is what you can offer beyond yourself.

The extraordinary story of Khalida Popalzai is, at face value, about developing a women's football team in Afghanistan. But look just a little deeper and her purpose becomes clear: giving voiceless women a voice. Although she loves football as a game, she has also used it to empower women, to improve their rights both in Afghanistan and globally:[16]

> I wanted to start a movement through football. Every human has a right to a voice, regardless of passport. I want people to see the world can be different. That is why I speak up.
>
> I believe everyone comes into this world for a reason, with a task we have to do. We have to use our opportunities to help change the world to a better place for every human being.

Khalida is only 32, and she's experienced levels of fear far beyond what most of us can imagine. But by having a purpose, she has been able to face down the hardest of challenges.

When Khalida was nine, living in Kabul, the Taliban announced girls would no longer go to school. 'This was during the dark period of the Taliban regime,' she says. 'Women had no rights. They were not allowed to work, to study or to participate in any social activities. Women had to cover themselves, to wear the burqa. They weren't allowed to leave the house without a man.'

Khalida is from an educated and well-travelled family. Both her grandmother and her mother worked, her mum as a PE teacher. For safety, and so Khalida could continue her education, the family left their home and country to live initially as refugees in Pakistan.

Five years later, when Khalida was 14, the Taliban lost power and the family returned to Kabul. But the influence of the Taliban regime lived on. 'Women and girls still lived in fear. There were limited social activities – women just went to school and back home,' she says.

Khalida loved to play football with her three younger brothers after school. But as she grew up and became more obviously a woman, the pressure from society grew for her to stop playing outside. 'People said I should belong in the home and the kitchen. To wait for a husband.'

Her grandfather, who she calls a 'well-travelled feminist', said to her: 'Don't wait around for a man to come and change your world and pick you. Be a fearless woman, be independent.'

Society said her life belonged to the men of her family. 'People thought I wasn't a good girl or woman, as I didn't walk, talk or behave in certain ways. Every day at school, other boys told my brothers that because I was playing football, I was like a prostitute. It made my brothers so angry they ended up in fights. As a girl child you are the honour of the family. That's a lot of fear to put on a woman or a girl. I questioned everything. I thought, who made these rules?'

Khalida and her mother saw football as a route to change. 'As football is seen as a man's game, it could send out the message that change is possible.'

They started a girls' football team at Khalida's school and began a campaign to get more women playing football, asking the Afghan Football Federation for support. The AFF said that women playing would bring shame on the country.

But Khalida and her mum persisted and in 2007, when FIFA announced funding for women's football teams, they got their wish. That year, the first ever Afghan women's team played their first tournaments, with Khalida as captain. There was still a lot of opposition to women playing football. 'It was tough. It was dangerous. We were attacked in the streets and at school. During training, men threw stones at us until we had to abandon the sessions.'

That abuse only strengthened Khalida's purpose. 'For me, being captain was not enough. Every night, when I turned on the TV, there would be news about women being stoned, about honour killings. It made me feel so disturbed. I felt guilty for not taking action. I couldn't ignore other women's situations. I chose football as a tool to raise my voice and be the voice for women in my country.'

Khalida lobbied for a job in the AFF. 'Because I saw that was the place the changes are made.' It took months but, aged 20, she became the first female employee.

By raising her profile, Khalida had to face even more hate and anger. 'It was tough for me to stand up alone to be the first person doing this. People were scared that their daughters would hear my voice and do what I was doing. By speaking up, I not only put my life in danger but my family's too. We received serious death threats. My family were attacked.'

In 2011, the situation escalated. Khalida was accused of being a terrorist and had to flee the country. At first, she lived in India and Pakistan, then travelled to Denmark, where she still lives now. 'I saw how tough it was to live in a refugee centre, where you have no idea about your future.' Her work helping the women in the camps became the beginning of her charity Girl Power, which campaigns and educates women through sport and football.

When Khalida left Afghanistan, the women's football team had stopped. Then, in 2016, the Afghanistan women's football committee asked her to help them re-establish the national team. Khalida and her management recruited players – both inside and outside Afghanistan – and raised funds. They held training camps outside the country, flying in all the players.

'The idea was to be a great example of a group of women supporting each other. Our dream was to see the national team play in the World Cup.'

They were moving towards that goal when, in 2018, some of the players, some even as young as 14, reported they'd been violently sexually assaulted and raped by the then president of the AFF, and sexually and physically harassed by some other AFF employees. Not living in Afghanistan, Khalida hadn't known this was happening.

'Instead of firing those men, the AFF fired nine of the players and accused them of being lesbians. That put those women's lives at risk,' says Khalida. 'It was horrible. We stopped playing – I didn't want to give those abusers even one day more to violate the rights of the women.'

This, Khalida said, was her lowest point. 'I felt broken, tired, alone. It was horrible to hear those stories. Even talking about them made me feel sick. So how must it have been for the women who experienced the abuse?'

Khalida and her team contacted international football federations for help but things moved slowly. They started their #Voice4voiceless campaign on social media. She'd just started a job at a Danish Superliga football club, FC Nordsjælland, and was convinced she'd be asked to leave because of her campaign. But the club told her they were behind her. It was this kind of reaction, she says, that helped her cope. 'The support of people, both men and women, who believed us and trusted and stood up and said we hear you, was so important to me.'

Finally, in 2019, AFF's ex-president Keramuudin Karim was banned from football for life by FIFA. Now, a year on, there is a women's league in Afghanistan and tournaments around the country, with over 3,000 women playing. 'Now, women's football is led by women. The women can play with no fear of getting abused or of being sexually harassed.

'I feel like the luckiest and most privileged person on this earth because I found the purpose in my life at a very early age. It came out of my fear that the world would continue in the same way. That fear made me stand up.'

Khalida says she'll keep working, for every girl somewhere who's ready to give up or who doesn't know that change is possible. 'How could I leave that girl there alone?'

Your purpose might be something you're in service of, something or someone you love and care about deeply, or it might be a call to action that you cannot turn away from. Your purpose isn't always about your day job. It is about where you spend your best energy and where you put your love. But it is going to feel so compelling that you want to give a significant part of your life and energy to it.

Your purpose doesn't have to be grand or dramatic, or on the world stage. Not everyone has to start a charity (although if that is your purpose, go for it!). Your purpose might be making other people laugh, for example. Or bringing people together in a community. I can see that my mum's purpose is unconditional love: to make everyone in our family and her friends feel really loved.

Also, unlike Khalida, your purpose may not be obvious. You don't have to know your purpose at age six or 16 and stay true to it for ever. It can evolve over time, from experience or after adversity.

When I work with people to help them uncover their purpose, I start by asking them to tell the story of how they got to be who they are today. As part of that, I might ask the following questions:

How did you decide what and who you care about most?

What experiences and beliefs shaped your ideas about life, and your values?

What has been consistent for you in your life, either non-negotiable or a regular pull on your attention?

What lessons from family or education anchor you?

What challenges have been important for you?

And what did you work out doesn't much matter?

Reflecting this way, on how you became you, will naturally bring up this last question:

How does this identity link to what you do with your life?

Sometimes there is a gap between what people are called to do and what they do today. This kind of purpose work can deepen your commitment to where you already are, or it can inspire change.

Free-diver William Trubridge, who we met earlier, was training for his deepest dive yet when he went on a coastal hike. He likes to walk to get rid of the build-up of lactic acid from his muscles, clear his head and, he says, 'draw energy from the sea'.

He felt his phone buzz in his pocket and absent-mindedly pulled it out. It was just an alert from Twitter: 'Sea Life is now following you.' But at that moment the wording struck a deeper chord:

> I have no pretensions that the ocean's sea life gives a damn about me jiggling around in the upper 1 percent of its depths, but I do give a damn about sea life, and I know that with every success I achieve in free-diving I secure more power and leverage to be able to influence the issues I care about. 'Do it for the oceans' is one of my greatest motivators, and so even the passing fancy that the ocean's sea life might have noticed my efforts and be interested in them added to that motivation.

As with Khalida, a pull towards your purpose is a pull away from fear and conformity. And in times of fear, you can draw on your sense of purpose. It provides you with a motivation that's more compelling than your compulsion to quell the fear. So it gives you the strength to stick with what's scaring you, to step forward even if you are so frightened that you feel frozen to the spot.

CHAPTER 16

Replace fear with surrender

Do you have a lucky charm? Something you wear to job interviews or dates, take to big games, or put on your desk for an exam? Maybe a necklace, a mascot, even a pair of shoes?

When we're scared or nervous, we often feel tiny and insignificant against fate. We crave support or someone on our side. We want to be held by forces bigger than ourselves, to have the burden of control lifted from our own shoulders, even just for a moment. I call this 'useful surrender' – and it is useful against fear.

Another version of this might be when you clench your fists and screw your eyes shut and wish hard for something, whether it's that the player you're cheering for scores, the test results are clear or the email has the news you want.

Letting go and appealing or trusting something bigger than us – which may be God, creative forces, or the power of collective energy – has psychological value. And it relieves tension. It can be helpful to recognise or even just to hope that there are other forces at work in your life – whether it's nature or will – and not that everything that happens is because you made it happen.

Why surrendering works

Surrender may or may not be a natural part of your culture and faith. But for all of us the idea of some kind of unknown can be of great value, especially in the face of fear.

Surrendering in this way is not about shrugging off accountability for your own actions or making excuses. It is about opening to the possibility that you are not all there is. You are leaving room for a little mystery and a little divine intervention, whether you are a believer or not. And when you consider that human emotion is a lot stronger than human reason, this kind of surrender to mystery starts to make sense.

In football, Argentinian forward Lionel Messi is a hard worker and one of the greatest talents the sport has ever seen. You'd assume he'd be the last player to need extra help. But in one critical moment, Messi demonstrated surrender in action. After he missed a penalty in Argentina's 1–1 draw in the group stages of the 2018 World Cup, journalist Rama Pantarotto gave Messi a red ribbon for luck. It was one his own mother had given him.

In the press conference after Argentina's match with Nigeria, Pantarotto asked Messi if he'd worn it. Messi pulled down his sock to show him the ribbon, tied around his left ankle.[17] 'You're joking. OK, well someone is about to have a heart attack. I mean it. Wait, you scored with your left foot?' said

Pantarotto . . . 'No, you scored with the right foot.' 'Doesn't matter, it helped,' replied Messi.

That is the key: not that it 'worked' but that it 'helped'. It's not about the object or whether it carries magic but that in Messi's mind, it gave him more resources. The upshot? He had even more confidence.

The air crews who flew in the Lancaster bomber squadrons in the Second World War also used useful surrender. These men faced conditions that incited tremendous fear, every time they flew. This is wireless operator/air gunner John 'Ginger' Stevens talking about his experiences, in the documentary *Battle Stations: Lancaster Bomber – Target Germany*: 'You were at the beginning of an adventure. You were at the beginning of something dangerous. You were at the beginning of fear and you would feel fear. Anyone who said they didn't feel fear were liars or nuts . . .'

The crew had to find a way to adapt to this pressure, to cope. Some of them used imagination and a sense of the mysterious. One way was the good luck charm, similar to Messi's ribbon. Stamper Metcalf (Bomb Aimer) says: 'I got married three days before D-Day. I had a silk stocking from the wife. I tied that around my neck and I never took that silk stocking off until I'd finished ops. I showered with it. I did everything. It was my lucky charm was that silk stocking.' And Bob Pearson (Rear Gunner) says: 'One or two of the crews from the squadron were given dolls by a young girl who used to knit them as mascots. I carried that doll on all the trips I did. I swear blind that mascot brought me back.'

Here is Ginger Stevens talking about the beginning of a mission. This kind of surrender is to make the plane itself an entity with its own power and magic, its own will:

This is the moment of no return. The decision has been made. You are in her world now. And suddenly it all seems to happen. You have a full bomb bay, full power and suddenly she's let go. That moment is unbelievable! You roar down the runway and all you can hear is the noise, the noise – and it's a beautiful noise. You've got 1400 yards to lift about 14,000 lbs. It starts to seem that she's going to lose the game against gravity. But just after halfway you feel a gentle bounce and then another gentle bounce, and suddenly you're weightless and you're airborne. It's moments like that she tells you what she's all about. She's magnificent, just magnificent. She is magnificent – not it, she.

So while the risks of the crews' everyday existence were out of their control, they found safety in their imagination and belief in mysterious forces. The point is: if you feel the need to surrender to something bigger than you, then don't worry if it doesn't feel logical. Because that doesn't stop it being useful.

Letting go

Trusting in something bigger than you is one kind of useful surrender. But there's another kind of surrender that is useful against fear: letting go of control.

As you read in chapter 5, being in a fear-promoting environment can make us hold on more tightly to what we can control, whether that's ourselves or other people. We have a natural craving for stability, to know what's going to happen next and so, when we're fearful, it's an easy step to over-control.

But the reality is, holding on tightly is pointless. We can't ever get a real grasp on life, because it's always changing.

Perhaps your mantra in life is 'no surrender' and you're proud of the fact you never give in. You might think of this mindset as passionate and determined. And it could be. You can tell by asking this question: 'Am I trying to control my own effort or the outcome?' The former is a clue that you have a committed, passionate mindset but the latter means you might have an inflexible one.

An unwillingness to let go will sound like one of these: 'I am right and you are wrong'; 'This is what I want and nothing else will do'; 'My way is the only way.' If you hear yourself saying something like this, you are not leaving space for possibility.

If you need to be in total control, then when life inevitably gets in the way it will leave you feeling stressed, anxious, disappointed or frustrated. For example, if you are determined that your daughter should follow you and train as a doctor, you'll be devastated when she chooses to study accountancy.

If you are determined to stay in your comfort zone, naturally you will feel bad when you are forced out of it. For instance, if you can't consider applying for a new job, despite having outgrown the one you're in, being made redundant would feel devastating.

Control and comfort should not be the building blocks of your life; they make weak foundations. What do work are adaptability and resilience, because they allow you to try and risk failing, to learn from what you got wrong, or to try new things. Surrendering in this way is a way of turning down the ego, that part of us that thinks it can control all reality and protect us from pain.

It might sound difficult, but it is really about letting go, instead of always struggling to 'do' something.

I remember standing on the sideline at a big game. At a crunch point, I looked to my right, and noticed a colleague's fists so tight his knuckles were white, strain drawing his mouth into a hard line, no breath moving his chest. He was suffering, concluding it would go wrong before it had happened.

I looked to my left at another colleague. His hands were open on the metal railing in front of him, eyes focused but soft, his composed breath flowing in and out, almost smiling in appreciation of what he was witnessing. His trust in and empathy for the players was palpable.

The reason for the difference? The second colleague accepted he wasn't in control. He was comfortable not being able to influence the moment. Instead, he was able to surrender and accept it.

Culturally, we think there always has to be tremendous striving and tireless work to succeed. So, while the practice and training needed will be hard work, in order to excel, we need to let go.

This may sound flippant, but you need to think like a Jedi. As Yoda says in *Star Wars III Revenge of the Sith*, 'Do or do not, there is no try.' That's because surrendering lowers tension, lowers resistance and releases fear.

A young musician – a trumpet player – contacted me after the 2018 World Cup and asked if she could come and talk to me about ways to deal with her performance fear. A rising star in a field where discipline and perfection are revered, she felt she'd lost her confidence in big performances, under her fear of making mistakes. We went through the basics of her emotional management and pre-performance routines – techniques similar to those in chapter 8. And we talked about how she could stay composed in the time leading up to her taking her seat in the orchestra. But something was still not right.

I asked her to tell me what the music felt like.

'Feels like? Well, I kind of hear it rather than feel it. But I guess my mouth feels it, the vibration of my lips inside the trumpet mouthpiece. I guess my fingers feel it, the pressure between my fingertips and the tops of the valves. Actually, I guess my ears feel it too, the pitch and tone of a good note or a bad one. Now you mention it, my whole body feels it – I can feel space in my back ribs and the rise and fall of my stomach as I breathe. I can feel my legs and arms taut and engaged. And I can feel the resonance of all of the other sounds of the orchestra through my feet on the floor.'

'So how does the music get made?' I asked. 'Do you make it, or does the trumpet make it?'

She considered this for some time. 'We make it together. It comes through me, but the music already exists – it just needs me to breathe and enable it to come to life.'

'So the more open you are, the easier it is for you to pass the music in to the trumpet?' I asked. 'So you can create together?'

'Yes, yes that's a hundred percent right. It always flows best when I am open. I hadn't really considered it as creating together until now.'

'So the onus for perfection can't really be all on you and your ability to execute the music. It sounds more like your job is to stay open?'

'It really is.'

'And what do you want your audience to feel when they listen to your music?'

'I want them to feel joy and energy and be filled with emotion.'

'What a wonderful gift. Could it be that they are also part of the creation?'

'My audience?' She paused. 'Well, yes. I suppose that if they don't feel the emotion, then there is a lost connection. If I am fully connected to the music, the audience will feel it too.'

'Thinking of your performance this way, how might you adapt the way you look at your fear?'

'I think it takes up too much space! It is better to have more space inside me for the music to flow. I should focus on making space for the music, not just on what's going on in my own head. I will enable the music to come through me.'

This seemingly small surrender has made a big difference to the musician's sense of involvement with and fulfilment in what she is doing.

Her craft will always need precision and discipline and mastery, but her overly rigid and controlled approach was creating tension and anxiety. When she could let go and open up, her tension lowered and so did her nerves.

Allow your emotions

Finally, there's a third kind of surrender. And that is letting emotion itself move through you.

So many people facing fear tell me they might feel it pushing against their chest or tightening their throat. But then they squash it down and swallow it, in order that no one sees it.

Repressing emotion is a culturally learned behaviour. It has been especially encouraged in boys and men, who have often been conditioned to believe that showing fear is a sign of weakness. But it has consequences. If you do this regularly enough, your fear can stay twisted up inside you and important-antly, people who care about you can't know how you are doing.

It's one thing to hold back emotion at the moment you're facing down an opponent in the boxing ring, for example. But there are times and places you *should* let down your guard. How much better do you feel after a good cry? If you haven't done it for a while, try it! I can assure you, I've known the toughest of the tough to cry. And without the cultural con-straint of seeing it as weakness, it is sometimes just plain useful.

Instead of a good old cry, you could try screaming, roar-ing, head-banging heavy-metal style, stomping, or singing ridiculously loudly. Anything to allow the emotion to flow through you rather than stay jammed up. In children, these kinds of emotion-releasing behaviours happen spontaneously (maybe not the head-banging), but as adults we talk ourselves out of surrendering to them in case we look stupid or weak. It's your choice whether you want to share the experience with anyone else or not.

Emotional energy is fluid: it needs to move through you. Help it out.

CHAPTER 17

Replace fear with dreams and desires

This is not a fluffy, romanticised suggestion that you 'follow your dreams'. It is far more practical than that: dreamers have a particular mindset that's useful against fear. They have the ability to move obstacles to get to their dreams. They're more open to failure, restarting, disappointments, knock-backs and doing what it takes to succeed.

Dreams aren't given the status they merit. We talk about day-dreamers as having their head in the clouds, about dreams being for romantics and fantasisers. In comparison to plans, which have a concrete, solid reputation, dreams are seen as flawed and vague.

But think about this: what comes before a plan? A dream, almost always. They're not something to shut down. They won't stop our progress; in fact, they do the opposite. And dreamers are far from being wrong-headed. Rather, their dreams come from a lust for life. Dreams are the basis for living with soul and substance.

To see dreams in action, look at the career of footballer and England captain Harry Kane. After starting at Tottenham Hotspur youth academy at the age of 16, he was promoted to the senior squad. He said: 'I'd love to be captain of Tottenham and hopefully England as well.' And later on he reflected: 'To go out at Wembley and score is what you dream about as a kid.'

None of those outcomes looked likely for a few years. Harry spent his early career out on loan to a series of clubs lower in the football pyramid. Eventually, five years on, he got his chance to play for Tottenham. In his debut senior season he scored a whopping 31 goals. Despite that, the story that went alongside him was that he was a one-season wonder, had no left foot, could only score from tap-ins and didn't have the quality expected of a world-class player.

Harry doggedly refused to give up his dream. The result? Among other career highs, in the 2018 World Cup, he was awarded Golden Boot for the most goals scored. And in 2019 he was anointed as Tottenham's third-highest all-time goal scorer. Dreaming gave him his North Star to follow.

Why is *desire* included along with dreams here? It's a vital part of that equation because its intensity can match that of fear.

You could describe desire as our wilful fantasies about what life could be like. Psychotherapist Dr Mark Epstein, author of *Open to Desire*, has a nice way of describing how important it is in our make-up: 'Desire is the juice. It's how we discover who we are, what makes a person themselves.'[18]

Desire can push us to overcome resistance and stumbling blocks – and our natural tendency to stay with the status quo. Most of us are more swayed by the fear of loss than the hope of gain. Generally, we'd rather protect what we already have than take a risk to get something we want.

It's a trait that's hard-wired in our old brain circuitry. We're particularly afraid of letting go of what we have prepared for, or committed to. For example, say you're a lawyer with eight years' investment in your studies, training and work experience, but you really want to become a ski instructor. However unhappy you are, that investment of time, effort and money will make it harder for you to switch careers.

We hang onto what's bringing us success as well as what isn't. It takes something compelling – such as desire – to compete with this tendency to stick with what we know.

How desire works

You have around 60,000 thoughts a day, and they'll mostly be coloured by fear or by desire. Both of these can motivate, but fear does so by making us want to escape what we don't want, while desire pulls us towards what we do.

For example, a desire-driven thought might be: 'I'm going to order that delicious-looking salad.' The fear-driven version would be: 'I'd better have a salad as I don't want to put on weight.' It may sound like a tiny difference: you're still eating the salad. But the tone of your thoughts will determine how you see the world.

You might want to be careful to direct your desire too, or it can take you in a less fulfilling direction. Desire can fuel a desperate kind of ambition that's very different from a soul full of dreams. This kind of ambition can come with ruthlessness, a greedy desire to be rich or powerful or personally acclaimed, the essence of winning shallow.

Ambition has some of the same great qualities as dreams, but it can come with narrow focus and the fear of missing out. That's why desire works best combined with dreams: dreamers don't pin their expectations on single outcomes, they just decide to leave nothing out there on the journey.

Let's go back to Lee Spencer, the ex-Marine who rowed the Atlantic. Twice. His motto is: 'Dare to dream, and if you don't fail you're not dreaming big enough.'

If you still think that the idea of having a dream is a little vague or wishy-washy, Lee might convince you otherwise. He says:

I believe in dreaming when you can guarantee you'll fail at the first attempt. The failure is integral to the success. If you achieve without failing, what success was it really? Success is only worthwhile if it comes at the end of a lot of failures. Otherwise, it's cheap success.

I wanted to be in the Marines for as long as I can remember. When I was 13 years old I went to a career fair. I went straight up to the bloke in the Marines and told him. He asked me if I was captain of my football team and I said, 'No, I made the B team.' He asked if I was captain of my rugby team and I explained we didn't have one at our school.

He said, 'What we are really looking for are people who are captains and sportsmen. So you're not really what we're looking for.' I asked him for one of the brochures anyway. He said, 'No we haven't got any left.' I looked behind him, and there was a big pile of them.

Aged 18, I went to the careers office. The bloke said, 'You're not quite there. We don't think you'd pass our potential recruits course.' I took that as fact. I saw Royal Marines as superhumans, which I'm not. But I did not lose the dream.

Three years later, the night before I left to do my potential-recruits course for selection – a massive hurdle – my uncle said to me: 'Ha, you won't get in. You won't be able to put up with the discipline, people telling you what to do.'

I used all three of those knock-backs as an energy. But it was the dream of being in the Marines that directed that energy. The dream turned blind ambition into the possible.

The rest is history: a 24-year career including three tours of Afghanistan. You can see that for Lee his dreams gave him a firm hold on his vision for the future. Dreams are laced with imagination. While knowledge is powerful perhaps imagination, with its unending possibilities, is even more so.

Lee lost his leg below the knee in a freak accident, when he stopped to help a family who'd had an accident on the side of the motorway. Another car crashed into the one he was helping and he was hit by an engine block. The force completely dislocated his left knee and almost severed his right leg below the knee:

When I was alone on the edge of the road, I made the decision not to call my wife Claire to say goodbye. If I had made that call, that would have been an admission that this was it. If I'd have called I don't

think I'd have been here. Losing your leg or dying is
a serious occupational hazard for a Marine in
Afghanistan. So you think about it, make peace with
it and put it to the back of your head.

At this point, Lee decided to live rather than to capitulate to
fear. 'It wasn't a shock. It was like, all right, leg's gone. Now I
have got to stop the bleed. I don't think that's necessarily a
normal response.'

By the time a guy called Frank and his daughter Zeneli
came to help Lee, he'd lost so much blood he knew he was on
the edge of life and death. 'I could feel all the classic symptoms
of deep shock and I knew that I had minutes or less to do
something. I wasn't feeling fear at that point at all.'

'I got Zeneli to stand on my femoral artery on my groin,
to put all her weight on her heel to try and shut the blood
down. And it worked.'

The fact he survived the accident was extraordinary.
But his recovery, and what he's achieved since, has been even
more so:

My life was overtaken with an absolute desire to get
better, to walk. Every day there was real tangible
progress. I remember going down to the shop in the
hospital for the first time and how great that felt. Then
getting out of hospital. Then getting out of the
wheelchair. Then walking, then going further, walking
more easily. While I was still in hospital, I challenged
myself to run a marathon within a year. Doctors said
this would be unlikely – probably impossible – because
my left leg was so badly damaged from the dislocation.

I set lots of little challenges, like a goal of raising £10,000 in the first year for charity. I started with a one-mile sponsored walk in London. Then a walk up the rock of Gibraltar. My aim was to get better. But it was a good opportunity to also do some good out of a shitty situation. And setting a public goal is like playing a trick on yourself; it forces you not to give up.

Then there was an Atlantic row with three other servicemen who were also amputees, followed by his solo row:

I am thrilled to be able to raise money for the charity but fund-raising wasn't the point. My desire was to make sure my own identity wasn't defined by what happened to me, or by having one leg. It would be arrogant to say, 'I can do this, why can't you?' I don't want to inspire or, worse, judge other people who have disabilities. I have advantages, contacts, I've been gifted opportunities so it was a lot easier for me to make it happen. What I say now is: no one has to accept someone else's label.

If you can couple a dream with the magnetic force of desire, as Lee has done all his life, it will help you shape your goals, make choices and actions – and you'll feel fully alive. It may feel scary at first. The trepidation of pursuing a dream might seem similar to fear. But because there's no negativity, what you'll feel will be closer to excitement and the thrill of the chase rather than dread.

Being inspired by your dreams will also make you more willing to step over any fears – as well as other barriers – in the way of what you want. Those barriers include rejecting the status quo, thinking small and believing there's not enough success to go around. When you want something badly enough, you'll be prepared to do what it takes in ways that might even seem loopy to the next person. Your desire will bring energy, work ethic and will to the dream. And once this becomes equal weight to the fear, it topples it. That is even if, along the way, you fail and fail and fail some more.

This is what Dame Jane Goodall, the iconic conservationist and primatologist, was talking about when, in a 2015 speech,[19] she described the 'indomitable human spirit' that we all have inside us:

> Every single one of you, of us, has the same indomitable
> spirit. We just have to learn to free it, to follow it, to
> trust in it, to follow where it takes us. To lose fear and
> go out there and do what our indomitable spirit would
> like us to do. That's what we can all do. That's how we
> can make the world a better place.

You don't have to be a great spirit, someone rare and special to follow your dreams. We all have what it takes.

CHAPTER 18
Replace fear with real connection

Who are your people? The people you can turn to, who truly know and accept you?

This is important: being known and feeling you belong are fundamental human needs, not just nice-to-haves. Life isn't just about who you are, it's about *whose* you are. We're never self-contained individuals in our own little worlds, we are social animals. We don't thrive and (as children, at least) we may not even survive without relationships.

In fact, belonging may be the strongest psychological desire we have. In this chapter, I'll explain how it also might be the most important one for coping with intensely painful emotions, including fear. It's so critical to us that we even fake fitting in, and mimic other people in order to be accepted. You might have done this by staying silent about your values or views or by adopting other people's.

Belonging weaves a safety net around you, brings you comfort, confidence and happiness. Everyone needs someone they can turn to when things get rough, when you're sad or angry or afraid. Belonging is also an incredible fear-fighter. And one that brings results. Because it allows you to take risks, knowing you'll be loved regardless.

If you listen to an acceptance speech at an awards night, almost without fail there will be a little nod to someone who allowed the winner to feel seen, who gave them a place to be real, who connected to them as the imperfect and wonderfully flawed human being they are. It may have been the kit man, team doctor, teacher, best mate or teammate. Whoever it was, it's the quality of intimacy that so often turns out to be the key that unlocks a fear-free and therefore excellent performance.

Keeping intimacy away

We're built for connection. We have deep social intuition. We can read each other without speaking and we can read what's going on in a social environment. We can feel another person's energy or mood without them saying a thing, and we can predict others' hopes and fears, largely because we often share them. Neuroscience is only just starting to understand our capacity for this kind of empathy.

So why do we avoid connection? Why do we have impersonal interactions with no eye contact? Why do we time our text messages to protect ourselves from seeming too eager or interested? Why do we hold back our feelings because we don't want to seem overly emotional or gushing?

The last time you had a difficult conversation with a colleague, did you really connect, look at them, show them how you felt, act as yourself? It's not what's usually done. But when we silence our instincts for intimacy, instead of feeling good about ourselves we feel alone and unknown.

We keep quiet because our cultural belief in 'the individual' tells us that each of us must stand on our own feet, be independent, not be needy. But this closes off the emotional connections that we need. So instead of being part of a community, the way human beings evolved, we often rely heavily on one or two people for support and affection, perhaps a partner or best friend. Beyond that, we stay private. The result, according to author Johann Hari, is even while we're surrounded by other people, we feel isolated, lonely and afraid, especially men. 'Loneliness hangs over our culture today like a thick smog,' he writes.[20]

How belonging works in action

The three door-openers to belonging are friendship, kindness and intimacy. Together, they allow a person to build a sense of identity that says, 'I can belong here.'

While most people accept the first two are important, intimacy has been sidelined. And the trouble is, it's this kind of deep connection that's one of our best allies in being able to face and replace fears.

Intimacy is the quality that's created when we get to know what each other is really like. It's way riskier than sharing the controlled set of facts about ourselves, the window dressing that we trot out most of the time.

Having spent most of my career in male sports teams, I can confirm that yes, the idea of intimacy as a way to overcome fear has raised eyebrows. Teamwork and bonding? No problem. Unity 'for the shirt'? No problem. Really getting to know each other? Wow.

You – like plenty of the players I worked with – might assume that the dog-eat-dog competitiveness between team-mates would make intimacy impossible. You might also assume intimacy would get everyone too emotional, leave them too unravelled. Both are myths.

You can grow intimacy one-on-one, but also in a group environment: a team, your workplace, relationship or family. It's about how to develop real, sustained closeness rather than flash-in-the-pan teamwork or just living side by side.

How to develop intimacy

Intimacy develops slowly, as we listen to each other and reveal who we are. Perhaps it requires us to show parts of our thoughts, circumstances and experiences that we'd rather no one else saw. And it also requires us to be willing to be present for others to do the same.

The most incredible example of this was an Australian rules football club I worked in, the Richmond Tigers. The season after I left the leaders decided to dedicate even more time and energy to connecting. Although they'd used psychological tools and analysis previously, it wasn't until this point that the big shift happened.

The Tigers, like most teams, were great people who were organised, obedient and dedicated. But obedience comes out of fear and respect rather than love, and the dedication was to an idea rather than to each other. The book *Yellow & Black* by Konrad Marshall tells the story of their monumental turn-around, how they won the 2017 Premiership breaking a

37-year drought. The Tigers is one of my favourite turn-around stories of all time because I know how much heart and soul went into it.

The coach Damien Hardwick introduced a vulnerability and bonding exercise called Triple H. He'd brought it back from a course on authentic leadership at Harvard. Triple H comes from the book *You Win in the Locker Room First* by NFL coach Jon Gordon.[21]

Building a successful Australian rules football team may not seem directly relevant to your life. But if you can build intimacy between 44 tough sport-playing blokes, you can likely do it anywhere.

In Triple H, you stand in front of the group and share three personal stories from your life: one of a hero, one of a hardship and one of a highlight. The coach took the lead, followed by the captain, Trent Cotchin. But over the course of the season, all 44 players did it.

Players told how they'd lost a relative, cared for a disabled loved one, overcome poverty or racism, and experienced joyful emotions like love and fatherhood. All aspects of human life, in fact.

As Konrad Marshall reports: 'These closed confessional sessions in front of 50 musclebound blokes often ended in a heady mixture of tears and applause and group hugging, and ultimately acted as emulsion, uniting the group en-route to a famous premiership.'

Running defender Brandon Ellis wept as he told his team-mates how he felt ashamed, 'like scum', growing up in a housing commission flat and stealing clothes from the mall. Veteran defender Bachar Houli spoke tenderly about how the birth of his daughter touched him, and how he now makes a point of kissing both his father and his mother every time he sees them.

Player Nick Vlastuin said he'd been 'shitting himself for weeks' before his turn came to stand up in front of and address his teammates. He spoke about his grandfather, a Dutch soldier in the Second World War who was imprisoned in Changi for four months before being sent to work on the Burma Railway.

This kind of vulnerability and bonding session has been dubbed 'a legal performance-enhancing substance' in the sports world. By unlocking the fear of being seen, it creates real unity. The exercise doesn't have to be Triple H, but it does have to have intimacy as its goal.

So how does intimacy lead to unity? Player 'Lenno' (Ben Lennon) explains one aspect in *Yellow & Black*: 'To know that the captain has the same thoughts as a second- or third-year player means everything. The idea that, "we're right here with you, we know you're doing it tough up there, talking about these things, but we're behind you." '[22]

Real intimacy is a special ingredient. It invests you in the group by lowering defensiveness and caution. It takes you beyond any fears of being exposed and removes pressure to look cool and some of the barriers that keep us separate.

It also prevents too much 'sheep' behaviour, where the flock follow the leader and never challenge because of the fear of not wanting to stand out and the shame-risk of saying something dumb. Knowing that you'll still belong if you stand out leaves more space for clear-headed thinking and smart risk-taking.

Above all, it inspires care and love. People learn from people they love. They can risk failing with people who love them.

Brandon Ellis wasn't sure the results on the field would have been the same without Triple H. In these sessions, he said, the players showed each other who they are, and why they are the way they are. 'We don't want to be fake,' Ellis says. 'We want you to know, "this is who the fuck I am". We've taken a massive step forward this year in how much we care. We're connected now.'[23]

There were other changes that helped the Tigers connect. Decisions were made in a more democratic way, taking the players' views into account. Leadership improved. There were mindfulness practice sessions, and coach and captain mentoring.

Another powerful contributor was the leaders themselves facing into their fears. Captain Trent Cochin kicked off 2017 with an unusual pre-season address to the players. One of the most admired and respected leaders in AFL, Trent decided to try something new. He told everyone how, vulnerable, hopeless and scared of failing he had been feeling after a disappointing 2016 season. He said he felt that he had it in him to be a good captain for them, but he needed to put it back to the group to make a choice:

A black cloud sat over my head for a big chunk of season 2016, in particular the back end of it. I'd never really shown that I was vulnerable in some way, especially as captain of a footy club. I [felt] free in 2017 based on that defining moment where I stood in front of 44 teammates, friends, peers and pour[ed my] heart out. It's something that I was petrified of doing but was also one of the most rewarding experiences of my life.[24]

At the end of his speech, every player embraced him. His authenticity opened the gates to intimacy, allowed the rest of the team to go there too.

A wider shift by the leaders addressed an identity issue for club and players that can perpetuate fear: racism. Racism is an issue in AFL just as it is in sport elsewhere and our wider societies, even if incidents of racism have diminished between players. In order to shift the views of the fans, the response of AFL clubs has often been to champion indigenous reconciliation and rights.

Each year there is a Dreamtime game on the same weekend in the season. That year, it was the 50th anniversary of the referendum in 1967, so was especially pertinent. Usually, in his post-match speech, coach Damien ('Dimma') wouldn't single out any one player. But this time, he showed his respect for player Shane Edwards, AKA Shedda or Titch. That day, Shedda was wearing the number 67.

Konrad describes what happened:

He [the coach] tells the group he appreciates what Edwards brings to the football club – what he has brought for 11 years now. He points out that including this Dreamtime game, Edwards will have played 192 games for Richmond Football Club – the most ever by an indigenous footballer.

'I love Shane Edwards,' he says, pausing and pointing to the small midfielder. 'And I want to see the love for Shane Edwards tonight because he's part of our family. Like Bachar. Like Lloydy is. Like Jack is. We do things for our family. We fight for them. We stand up for them. Stand up with Shane Edwards tonight.'[25]

He thus highlighted the intimacy, belonging and brotherhood between the indigenous and non-indigenous players.

Are you willing to share the real you? Unconsciously most of us just 'play on the surface' in groups, teams and even in couples, because we want to protect ourselves from rejection and pain. But this superficiality is an open door to more fear and loneliness. And a loosely bound couple or group, even when connected by a common purpose or cause, will buckle under pressure without intimacy.

How can you up your levels of intimacy? As a 'small I' introvert, I don't tend to enjoy large social groups and public outpourings of emotion. But what I do appreciate is the benefit of real intimacy. It is possible to become more intimate with people you don't know well just by being open-hearted and authentic, by saying what you mean. Speaking in a way that connects to people rather than alienates them is important (especially when you have 'Dr' in front of your name or a job title that may intimidate someone!).

Listening properly is too. That means so the other person knows you are hearing them rather than in a rush to be somewhere else. Showing care builds intimacy; offering genuine feedback about what you noticed in someone does too. But most of all, it's about not playing a role but just being yourself – whomever you are talking to.

You could also consider how much 'impression management' you are doing. Do you avoid saying that one extra thing on your mind – even to a dear friend or your partner – because you feel it's too personal or indulgent? Do you feel uncomfortable keeping eye contact if someone is complimenting you? How much self-regulation are you doing in your interactions to make sure that you influence someone's view of you positively? The irony is, people can usually feel how open or guarded you are from a mile off. And the smallest gestures of connection and intimacy can change the course of social interactions in big ways. If you can think of yourself as good enough, you won't need to hide as much. You may assume you need to feel safer in order to become intimate. But the paradox is, once you drum up the courage to go for it, the amount of safety it brings into a relationship or partnership or team is phenomenal. For most of us, intimacy and the caring it brings are untapped reservoirs of fear-busting and resilience.

CHAPTER 19

Replace pain with passion

Everybody will experience some level of struggle and suffering in their life. Everyone will face loss and grief, heartache and sadness. Pain – both emotional and spiritual – is an inevitable part of existence.

It can go two ways. Sometimes the amount of pain a person endures breaks them down. The result can be defiance, frustration, stroppiness, hatred or deep anger. When pain combines with fear, it becomes a force that can destroy you and your relationships.

But you can choose to take your pain down a different route, as the stories in this chapter show. There is a kind of alchemy that transforms pain and overcomes fear, and the ingredient that allows that shift is *passion*.

Joeli Brearley runs the UK charity Pregnant Then Screwed, which helps women with pregnancy and maternity leave discrimination, and lobbies for legislative change. She

founded it after she was sacked – via voicemail – when she told
her employer that she was four months pregnant. She says:

For at least two weeks, I was drowning in emotion,
cycling between anger, hurt and fear. It felt like they'd
kicked me in the teeth, at my most vulnerable. I was
terrified what this meant for my career. And whether I
could earn enough to keep a roof over my head. And
would I get another job, being visibly pregnant?

My friends and family gave me hugs and sympathy,
let me cry and rant and rave, which helped. My partner
let me do that for a bit, then said it was time to do
something. He encouraged me to apply for other jobs.
And I was lucky enough to find one that suited me
really well.

After I'd had [baby] Theo, I got severe postnatal
depression. I think being sacked contributed to that. In
those early months, I was bitter and full of revenge
plans. Whenever I met another new mum, I'd ask her if
anything happened about her job. Discrimination
during pregnancy, though illegal, turned out to be way
more common than I'd imagined; women who've been
bullied out, made redundant, or it's been made
impossible for them to work in some way.

Finally, a colleague said to me, 'you've got to let go
of this anger.' I realised the perfect way to do this would
be to channel my anger into helping other women. That
felt exciting. Now Pregnant Then Screwed has been
running for five years. We've helped so many women in
need, some who've even had miscarriages or ended up
homeless. I no longer feel angry about what happened

to me. The whole process has been incredibly cathartic. I feel a deep sense of comfort that I'm doing something positive.

You can choose to focus on changing or fixing or overcoming or addressing something – perhaps what you see as the source of your pain – rather than getting hijacked by fear. You can channel it into a raw passion, a passion to change something and a refusal to be silenced or stopped, despite fear.

For a textbook example, here is an excerpt from climate change activist Greta Thunberg's 'How Dare You' speech to world leaders at the United Nations in September 2019:

> This is all wrong . . . How dare you continue to look away and come here saying you are doing enough. The politics and solutions needed are still nowhere in sight.

The gap between the story that she was being told and her own experience felt vast; she was faced with the options of fear or fury in response. She chose fury.

How to use your passion

Passion adds intensity and chemistry to whatever we feel. It is a compelling energy that leapfrogs reason and thought. It is not just about falling in love or lust, and it's not always a force for good: it also exists with anger, hatred, aggression and having something to prove.

There is something formidable about people with the kind of pain that fuels passion. They are doers. They refuse to be pedestrian and conformist or have their fears domesticated and 'shushed' in the face of the kind of cultural or personal fear most of us would shy away from.

Anthony is co-founder of Penificent Publishing, which tackles social issues for young people via comics and workshops, among other routes. His passions are art and teaching inner-city children about how the world works, so they can make the good choices that he didn't. He says:

> Penificent shows kids the rules of life and what
> can go wrong in comic form. What I draw is raw
> because I've lived it. It's relatable to kids because they
> are living it too. I saw that kids like me, their role
> models are footballers or rappers or drug dealers and
> that's it. Looking at my past, I realised no one had
> helped me. There was no positive big brother telling
> me, 'Don't do this, man.' No one taught us anything,
> no one informed us. That is how kids are set up to
> fail. And I didn't want other kids to go through
> what I did.

What Anthony went through is this: fighting and stealing, being excluded from school and prison. The violence he saw affected his mental health. 'People in the area see a lot of crazy, unfiltered violence all the time. It messes you up, gives you PTSD.' He describes himself as being in 'survival mode' as a teen. Aged 15, he was stabbed:

> That was the first time I felt really scared and enraged.
> My adrenalin was pumping so much I was still trying
> to fight even though I was getting stabbed. That's a
> scary feeling. Imagine dying and all you have in your

head is anger. I was so close to dying, they put me in
an air ambulance and flew me to hospital. I was so
angry I tried to discharge myself and crawl out but
I collapsed.

Looking back, he can see his mental health was suffering but
he had nobody to talk to. In black and Afro-Caribbean culture, he says, mental health problems are stigmatised:

It's a silent weakness that you can't talk about. Do
you know how mad that is yeah, keeping everything
inside you? The only outlet you have is violence. You
think, fuck it, if someone does something to me, I'm
doing it back. I didn't care if I got shot. I didn't care if
I died. I was so low, it was a self-destructive depression.
Every day I was having dreams thinking I was going
to die.

Aged 16, Anthony went to prison, prosecuted for 'joint
enterprise' as he was present when a robbery was committed,
although he wasn't involved in the crime:

I asked the judge, 'How am I supposed to know what
joint enterprise is?' I don't care what the law says, it
wasn't fair. Imagine getting stabbed and going to prison
in the same year. In jail people asked me, 'Why are you
in?' And I said, 'I don't know, don't even know. I'm just
here.' That fucked with my head.

While he was in prison for a second time, aged 18, he read an
X-men graphic novel called *Mutant X*.

I used to think comics were geeky. Then I realised that Mutant X was about Martin Luther King and Malcom X, their story was encrypted in the story. I thought, I want to write a sick story like this for the UK. With black characters being the norm. That teaches the practical things about life, like to watch who's in your circle. That it's OK to just turn the other cheek. That there's a different narrative. That it's good to talk about your mental health. That you can get PTSD from seeing violence.

Leaving prison, Anthony started a digital media, art and design course, which is where he met his business partner for Penificent.

The first story I created, *Peace and War*, is about machines enslaving humans. The machines are the government and the humans are the working-class people. But you wouldn't know it unless you sat down and analysed it. I feel the reward of knowing that my comics help kids think differently. It's not about me any more, it's past that. It's about a generation. Having my own kid played a part in what I'm doing as well. I didn't want him growing up like I did. It's about kids waking up and knowing that this ain't the life for them. The more people I reach, the better.

A lot of us believe what Anthony learned as a child: that ignoring difficult emotions and not talking about our pain will keep us strong. In fact, the opposite is true. Pushing down pain leaves us in a state of fear, living with a sense of threat, always waiting for the next bad thing to happen.

Instead, ask yourself where you might find the 'golden thread' of value in your pain. Has it led you to understand something about yourself that boosts your resilience, will or wisdom in a way that wouldn't have otherwise happened? Has your pain uncovered something you care about? That's what happened to Anthony, who realised he didn't want kids to go through the pain he went through. Or has your pain helped you understand how common your experience is for others, made you want to give back to others in the same position?

When you are facing pain and all the powerful energy that comes with it, the challenge is to try to create the circumstances and opportunities where the pain can keep flowing until it moves through you.

Pain takes us down for longer periods when it lodges in us and doesn't fade or change. Talking about it can keep it moving. Expressing it in art, dance, sport or other physical activity can too. Even focused breathing can. Like Mischa's blotchy red spots of shame in chapter 12, pain needs outlets to avoid it getting stuck. Ask yourself if you are blocking the pain anywhere, and how it can move through you.

If you have pain, and you can find a way to channel it with your passions as Anthony did, you can turn it into a positive force. You don't have to be the next Greta Thunberg, or change the world, but you can use the power of passion to create change that means something to you.

CHAPTER 20

Replace fear with laughter

'I have a fear of elevators. I have started taking steps to avoid it.'

If the energy of fear drags you down into negativity and dread, the energy of laughter does the exact opposite. Because it's made up of silliness, contradiction and illogic, humour forces you to change your perspective to one that's more upbeat, even if this is only temporary. But in the face of adversity, that can be everything.

The last ten years in the life of Emma Campbell, 48, could be the plot of a movie: first a run-in with breast cancer when her elder son was six and her triplets were six months old. Splitting up with her partner just weeks before the diagnosis. Five years later, meeting her now-husband Dave – the day after being told she had cancer for the second time. Then, five years after that, finding a lump in her other breast as well as a secondary tumour in her lung.

Six months ago, Emma had part of her lung removed, then a mastectomy and reconstructive surgery. 'But despite everything that has happened, I laugh now way more than I ever did. Isn't that strange?' she says:

I was born with a feeling of worry and fearing death. And in my twenties and thirties, the weight of my anxiety and fear was crippling. I used to look at people throwing their heads back and guffawing and think, I just don't understand that. My children would say to me, Mummy, you don't laugh.

Then the worst did happen. And it happened again and again and again. And now I do laugh. Even though I might be knackered and it's not easy being a mum of four, I have real joy in my life. For me, humour is linked to self-esteem. As I've become more confident, my humour has naturally evolved.

Now I lean naturally towards lightness. On paper my disease is incurable but I'm happier than I've ever been. That is the gift from all of this.

For Emma, her new-found humour comes from closeness and relationships:

I'm not someone who finds joke-telling particularly funny but I love the shared banter I have with my close friends and with Dave.

In the year before I met him, I remember thinking, could I ever have a new relationship? And I wrote down a list of the attributes I'd like in a new partner: loyalty and passion for example. And I remember writing the word 'banter' a few times. I wanted to have that feeling of ease with someone, those shared asides you only get when you know the other person so well. Where even a raised eyebrow can make you smile. And that is exactly what we have.

Of course, sometimes it feels hard. I have been in the blackest place, convinced I only had limited time left. Recently, the relief of being alive and the enormity of what has happened to me, has hit me. When I run with my friend Bryony, we can end up either laughing hysterically or crying. Both are a release.

Some of what I find funny is quite dark – I've spent a lot of time having treatment in the past five years, so there have been a lot of hospital-based giggles. All those times Dave told me how sexy I looked in my white post-op compression stockings, for example.

I do feel incredibly lucky. The miracle of 2019 is that, four months after the lung operation, I found out that tumour was benign. Even more, the doctors now think the tumour in my second breast is another primary, not secondary.

I am so grateful for this life. I focus on the good, on saying silent 'thank yous' throughout the day, when I'm in the bath or making a cup of tea. Laughing and gratitude are my ways of growing from what has happened to me.

Psychologists have been trying to unpick exactly how and why humour works as a coping mechanism for fear, anxiety and stress. The pre-eminent researcher on humour, Professor Rod

Martin of Western Ontario University, Canada, has shown that humour operates in three major ways.

Firstly, it creates bonds between people, as Emma describes. Because what makes us feel threatened — her diagnosis and being in hospital, for example — can also connect us. Humour can do that instantly, while letting us know that our fellow human being has got our back when we most need it.

The second way humour works is less complex. It helps you avoid whatever subject is making you uncomfortable or worried or anxious or scared. If you've ever giggled or laughed at the point you're feeling most anxious, this is what you've been doing. You probably won't be able to work out why you laughed as there is no why. It's simply an effective way to dispel the tension built up by fear.

Lastly, you can use humour to take control when you feel scared, a deliberate fear-control response. Laughing in the face of fear, if you like. Choosing to use humour changes your cognitive processing so you have more mental room to cope. This is about a deliberate effort to occupy your mental space with something functional and close down the space for fear to overwhelm you. Using humour and laughing changes the emotional tone and incites a different spirit; fear looms large and forecasts doom, humour says 'here goes' with a grin. Because your thoughts affect your feelings, it's a useful thing to do.

This one-way humour is used in the Royal Marines, the elite fighting arm of the British navy. They have four stated core values: courage, determination, unselfishness and, lastly, 'cheerfulness in the face of adversity'. On the surface, it might appear shallow for humour to have such a big role in such a serious job, but humour is considered to be vital not only in building comradeship but in releasing pressure.

'Humour is extremely important to the operational effect-
iveness of the Royal Marines,' says retired Major Scotty Mills.
'A strong and unrelenting sense of humour is one factor that
allows the RM to come to terms with the dangers we face.'

Scotty describes seeing humour at work:

I was part of a team in the arduous training in the very
north of Norway, in arctic and mountainous conditions.
The exercises are difficult enough – trekking in snow
boots, survival skills, creating shelters and snow holes,
learning how to get out if you fall through the ice. But
when you introduce temperatures almost always below
–30°C, each one becomes a survival situation that
requires not only team work but also psychological
strength.

One night, I was part of a patrol training exercise
where we had to ski 20km to conduct an enemy
attack. Our route back was across an open expanse of
frozen lake. As night fell, the temperature dropped
rapidly. Halfway across the lake, we stopped and
huddled for a navigational check. The section second-
in-command was using an anenometer, an instrument
that gauges the combined air and wind temperature
to measure the wind chill factor. He told us the
air temperature was –45°C and the winds were
50mph. So we were standing in a wind chill
factor of –76°C.

That is the coldest that I have ever experienced –
and ever want to. At that temperature, you have to
cover every part of your body. You even have to cover
your face with a mask to stop your spittle freezing and

your eyes becoming frozen together. A common phrase
we use in the Marines during these types of situations is
'remember who you are'. It reminds us that we are
Commandos and that nothing is impossible, no matter
how hard it is.

That night on the ice, we laughed off the danger by
sharing our dreams of eating juicy steaks and pizzas
washed down by copious amounts of beer, with lots of
banter about each other's crap pizza choices. No one
dared to show weakness by not joining in, otherwise we
knew it would have eroded our combined strength and
made us less robust and effective as a team.

Dark humour, adds Scotty, also helps shrink a difficulty in
your imagination, in even the most trying circumstances. This
story, from the IRA conflicts in the late 1980s, shows what he
means:

It was a live combat situation and a Marine had been
hit with a five-bullet spray. Incredibly he was unhurt –
but a bullet had knocked his false teeth and spun them
in his mouth. Despite having escaped death by a
fraction of an inch, he lay on the ground shouting 'man
down' with his teeth in upside down and back to front,
trying to make the onlookers laugh.

Due to his teeth being in wrong and his broad
Geordie accent, not a soul on the radio channel could
understand him. A group of locals came out to offer to
act as a cover. After a few minutes, the Marine got up
and ran past them and one kid shouted, 'You should be
dead, Mister!' The Marine replied, 'Marines never die!',

still running, still with his teeth in backwards. His humour broke the uncomfortable knowledge that one of our men was almost shot to death. That kind of unwavering cheerfulness in the face of adversity is part of a Marine's DNA.

Dark humour can sometimes make us cringe even while it makes us laugh. Also called black comedy or gallows humour, it can be morbid, graphic, edgy, even right on the edge of offensive. The subject matter is usually sensitive, possibly taboo. It may introduce humour where it's not expected, for example at a funeral or in the face of tragedy. 'Wow, how awful to lose a child. I wonder what the parents are going through.' 'Coffin brochures, probably.'

That doesn't stop it being effective in helping people deal with fear and stress, although not everyone likes it.

Trevor Noah, South African comedian, writer, producer, political commentator, actor and host of US satirical news programme *The Daily Show*, is a master of tackling sensitive subjects with this kind of humour.

He was born during the South African apartheid regime, a mixed-race child. This was his first joke, on his first show as host: 'I'm not gonna lie. Growing up on the dusty streets of South Africa, I never dreamed that I would one day have, well, two things really: an indoor toilet, and a job as host of *The Daily Show*.'

Using humour like this allows us (and him) to take a step back and look at situations that we might otherwise find easier to ignore, avoid or repress our feelings about. Make sure the humour you're using is the dark kind, rather than hostile. Because hostile humour – which is negative, aggressive and disparaging – isn't useful against fear. In fact, I suspect it creates more. It's when you get your kicks at someone else's expense and that damages them. Its energy is abrasive, can cross the line to becoming bullying or abuse.

When I was growing up, humour was one of the most important coping mechanisms in my family. You read a little about my non-picture-book childhood earlier in the book: I grew up with a single mum, very little money, drugs, alcohol and violence. But through the chaos, we always had humour.

There was the night I met my father for the first time, aged 14. Mum woke me up at 2 a.m. one day, saying, 'There's someone downstairs I want you to meet'. Strangely, I knew immediately who it'd be. Coming down the stairs in my pyjamas, I trembled with a mixture of dread and excitement. And as I walked into the room, I eyeballed my dad and said, deadpan, 'You owe me about twelve grand in pocket money.' That wisecrack made us both laugh, releasing the tension and creating a connection between us.

Reading the eulogy at my brother Gav's funeral was one of the hardest half-hours on one of the toughest days of my life. He killed himself at the age of 30, the end of a long struggle with mental illness and addiction.

I didn't want to be brave and I definitely didn't want to be standing up in front of all the people who'd loved Gav. I wanted to crumble. I wanted to find a hole to hide in and never leave it.

Humour came to my rescue. Instead of talking about the sadness, I told story after story of Gav's wayward ways. I told about when Gav swore blind that he had not graffitied on the side of the house . . . but the graffiti said, 'Gav was here'.

Another time, when he was around ten, Gav asked the old lady next door if he could borrow her lawnmower while Mum was at work, telling her it was to cut our grass. She thought: what a sweet boy. He then made her mower into a go-cart and held a street race. My flat-broke mum had to replace the mower.

There was a period of time in our family when domestic violence reigned. On one particularly crazy night, Mum's deranged recently ex-partner threw a hand-grenade through her bedroom window. She wasn't doing too well mentally at the time, so I was sleeping in her room. The grenade smashed through the window and woke us up. I looked at it, realised what it was and literally dragged her and my siblings down the stairs and into the back garden by their necks, clothes, whatever I could get hold of, in a frenzy.

The grenade didn't explode — it turned out to be a dud. After a few minutes in the cold, Mum looked at me and said, 'OK, Steven Seagal, can we go back to bed now?' We absolutely howled. In this ludicrous, bizarre and incomprehensible situation, humour was the best response to deflate the tension.

Psychological research shows that positive humour is actually even more useful than dark humour in helping you reinterpret a situation. Being able to laugh at your own seriousness, like Mum making us laugh at what (happily) turned out to be my huge overreaction, is especially useful.

If you can find a way to reframe the absurdities and difficulties of life, it's a brilliant strategy against fear. If wit isn't your particular gift, can you simply allow yourself some more *silliness?* It's a great form of fear-lowering vulnerability.

Allow yourself to be amused, or to amuse others, without managing your impressions or chastising yourself for being immature or foolish, or worrying about looking uncool. A child laughs with such abandon, with their whole body, it's a travesty we feel the need to be more 'grown up' and shut out that joy. Let yourself giggle until you snort and you can't use your squeaky voice to explain what on earth is wrong with you.

If you can learn to be playful, it'll have a beneficial impact not only on your well-being, but also on resetting your perspective and de-pressurising from fear. The upshot? If you want to change the mood quickly, indulge in a little bit of genuine, unscripted fun. Have a laugh.

Conclusion

What connects us

The ideas you've just read are to help you consider what might work for you, so you can move away from negativity and fear. They will enable you to explore and experiment with what feels fulfilling, and with what kind of potential you think you have.

Across your life you are likely to find different things useful. Perhaps at one point you'll see that you're not clear enough on your purpose, so you could focus on that. Or it might feel right to stop presuming everything is down to you, that you can let go or trust a little bit in the universe. Or that you need to up your vulnerability with other people in order to make deeper connections.

In fact, if you look at the ways the people whose stories I've told have replaced fear, most of them have something in common . . . and that is other people.

In Part 1, I shared ways that fear culture separates us from other people, by making us think we are in a survival-of-the-fittest face-off, battling them for success because there's not enough to go around. The *not-good-enough* fears and behaviours that are the result of this, in Part 3, keep us separate too because they leave us judging people, trying to control them, being jealous, not showing up as our real, whole selves.

Now, finally, I hope the section you've just read — or one of the chapters, at least — has helped you see a new way forward. Specifically, these stories show people getting over the root fear of being abandoned, which required them to treat relationships with a spirit of investment and generosity, find ways to help other people and the world beyond their own window, and look outside themselves for love, connection, laughter and purpose.

Hopefully, I've given you a set of ideas you can return to, each time you need to relook at your fear.

Fear is going to pop up in your life regularly and, when it does, you'll need to deal with it. Because fear will rarely just go away on its own.

While the sadness of a broken relationship can melt in due course, and the disappointment of failing can mellow, fear will stick around. No matter how much you try to ignore it, at best it will only shrink and rob you of satisfaction and fulfilment, but at worst it will make your life not your own. That's because fear is greedy for your attention and energy and resources.

If you've picked up this book, it's likely that all the strength, talent, potential and possibility inside you is protesting at being caged in by fear. You feel as if you have more life to live and give, more expanding to do, more of your wildness to let out. You're ready to win deep.

Fear is the barrier stopping you accessing this mental freedom. And that's why it's worth reckoning with, even though this won't be easy or instant. Now you've started to look at how much fear is costing you, you'll find you have more of your precious mental and emotional energy to put elsewhere, on things that don't drain you but make you stronger.

My challenge to you is to keep making sure your fear isn't running you. Mental freedom from fear is a choice you can make more often than you might think.

You'll feel relief from removing the weight of suffering under fear's influence. That is the suffering I have described as winning shallow – always comparing, striving to dominate, scared of failing, avoiding rejection and never feeling fulfilled, no matter how much your life looks like a success.

The way to do that is to See, Face and Replace. You might find it useful to think of shedding your fears as if you were a snake shedding its skin. As a snake grows, their skin stretches and no longer fits. In the same way, your old ideas and behaviours won't always grow with you.

While the old skin is getting uncomfortable and tight, a new layer of skin is developing underneath. Similarly, as soon as you have decided your fear of not being good enough is no longer serving you, there will be a new perspective forming under the surface, something more vibrant and a better fit with where you are today.

To leave the old skin behind is an effort for a snake, and it will be for you too. When a snake is ready to shed the old layer, it creates a rip or tear in the old skin by rubbing against a rough, hard object like a log or a rock. So too, I hope, all the stories you've read in this book have helped you create a 'tear' in your old logic that was keeping your fear alive, or in the old excuses that were stopping you from changing.

This process isn't a one-time thing. Just as the snake will have to shed its skin again and again during its life, your psychological growth and dealing with *not-good-enough* fear occasionally will be a constant right up until you're checking out.

You might have to shed more often at the beginning of a journey, as a young snake does, but you will have to keep shedding. And if you can decide that each time fear pops up or builds up you will shed and replace it rather than shut it down, you'll cause yourself a lot less suffering along the way. And you'll be set up to win deep.

Fear from the outside

I have written a lot in this book about what you, as an individual, can do about your fear. And in fact, a lot of 'performance psychology' focuses only on the individual or what goes on in your close relationships.

As you now know, fear isn't just in your own head. Certainly you will manufacture and recycle a lot of your own fear, but you're not doing it in isolation.

This focus on the self goes along with the hyper-individual culture we have developed in the last century or so – the idea that the journey of life is largely a personal one and that the only way to view the world we live in is from the inside looking out. The problem with this perspective is that it can shame and blame you into feeling personally flawed when you are overrun by emotions. It puts the burden on you alone to address this. It says that you need fixing, or that you're lost.

But you're not lost like a £10 note left behind in a back pocket of an old pair of jeans. You are real and complex; pretty similar to the rest of us. It's not just a 'you' issue, it's an 'us' issue. Your mess is our collective mess.

The trouble is, when we are fearful, we're less likely to reach out and connect, to turn to the next person for help. We tend to close down our connections. But rather than staying in the bubble of you, part of the solution is turning towards each other. One of the main ways out of fear is to be able to create intimacy or break down the barriers of connection.

That's why you'll have seen this theme come up so often in the stories of change: Jacques when he managed to find a way back to his daughter Emilie; Lee when he called his colleague Scotty at a low point during his Atlantic row, Khalida saying that the support of her club and others meant so much to her. That's because other people are where we get our real strength, and relationships are our ultimate fear-buster. They are at the heart of our ability to face into any kind of adversity or change – and, of course, fear.

The most powerful way through shame – which haunts all of us to some degree as either the desire to hide from life or the need to relentlessly prove ourselves – is to be *recognised*. To know that you can show yourself as you are, be seen and accepted.

You'll have read about this happening to, for example, Emma with Dave her husband, Jake with his parents, and the Richmond football players. This recognition or 'witnessing' happens when we can get outside our own bubbles. When there is a doorway open to love and connection.

This book is a compassionate conversation with you, and a challenge to turn towards others. It's not all up to you and happening inside you. So you don't need to sort it all out on your own. We are part of a common humanity, more similar than different.

So what is my final message? It is that love is stronger than fear. Choose love as your source of courage for your journey. If you can do that, you cannot fail to fear less and win deep.

A Fear Less Manifesto

This is not a roadmap but a set of ideas. Not just a set of ideas but a way of being.

And this isn't about being perfect. Hopefully we've established that perfection is a rubbish ideal. It is about freeing yourself up from incessant, draining negativity so that you can explore and experiment a bit more with what might feel fulfilling to you, and what kind of potential you really have.

You'll recognise fear when it's obvious; in a crisis, a tragedy, or a threat. But know that it also comes up in not-so-obvious ways. These hidden fears, based on what *might* happen or what *did* happen, are the root cause of much of your emotional suffering in life. They are stealing your fulfilment and peace every day.

As you now know, the best way to deal with any difficult emotion — in particular fear — isn't to try to smother or squash it, but to acknowledge it with courage. You need to honour yourself by being honest about the emotion, rather than avoid it or be embarrassed by it. And, of course, to engage with it so it doesn't take over.

That's not to say fear is the enemy. It is simply part of life, part of who we are in the same way that we also experience sadness, anger or heartbreak.

Remember: fear is coming from all around you. Our minds are always ready to create fear, and it's also coming from our beliefs and from our cultures too. We are always recycling fear. Have a look at what's going on around you, at home, at work, in your teams or groups or friendships. Listen to how people talk and relate. Notice how often fear is running the show.

Once you start to see fear in action, you can challenge it.

Dealing with in-the-moment fear

You will need to boss it and act straight away. The longer you leave it and the more space you give it, the harder it is to combat. The key is not to ruminate, to just do it. This is a time when you can use techniques. There are three 'umbrella' behavioural techniques: you can deploy whatever combination works for you, and vary them at different times.

1. Rationalise it

Use your logic to calm your catastrophising. Talk to yourself – you can write a version that has meaning for you. Some examples:

> 'You are ready for this, just like you were yesterday.'
> 'You've done this 1,000 times before, and you only needed to do it 200 times to be ready.'
> 'According to the stats it's a very low probability that it will go wrong.'

'The likelihood of it being an intruder is minimal, and the
    alarm is on.'

'There are no snakes here — it is probably a squirrel I can hear.'

'The guy driving is trained and capable and knows what he's
    doing.'

'So many people have come through this well before.'

2. Distract yourself from it

Again, find what works for you. You can listen to music or TV
or radio or podcasts. You can make contact with others,
engage your imagination in something else (like a game),
engage your cognition in something else (like Sudoku).

3. Process it

Use breathing exercises to calm yourself physically and emotionally. Visualise a positive outcome, use an affirmation or
prayer. Do muscle relaxation exercises.

Dealing with *not-good-enough* fears

Seeing your fear

Start to build up a picture of your fears.
Ask yourself: who or what stirs up fear in you? When and
where does this happen? In what kind of situations? And
what would be the worst thing that could be exposed about
you? Fears may appear as: perfectionism, keeping parts of
you hidden or yourself separate, staying small, critical judgements of yourself and others. Underneath all your fears is
the fear of not being good enough, of being cast out and
'abandoned'.

It's going to take the courage to be vulnerable to admit fear.

Say 'I think I am behaving in this way . . .' or 'I'm recycling this behaviour pattern . . .' or 'I'm repeating this mistake . . .' or 'I'm avoiding this opportunity . . . because underneath I am feeling fear.' If you think fear is weakness, you may have a blind spot around it. But it's more important to overcome fear than to blindly push through and ignore yourself.

Fear likes to stay hidden.

You might think you're worried about messing up your presentation and looking like an idiot in front of your colleagues or your boss – but underneath that worry, maybe you're afraid they'll realise you're not good enough and not up to the job. Or you might be afraid the study choices you make now won't line you up for career success – but underneath you're afraid of not meeting societal or parental expectations.

You have a secret weapon to help you fully see your fears and what they mean for you: your imagination.

Because of the god-like status we've given science, logic and reason, we've demoted and ignored our deep imagination as another source of information and wisdom. Fear comes with an energy that is forceful but not always able to be described with labels and logic alone. Using imagination lets you get much closer to the core of what is going on.

Look at how you recycle fear, too.

We tend to think of fear as an inside job, not understanding the role culture plays. There's a deeply ingrained if unspoken belief in our culture that fear is essential for success. But with an in-built biological and neurological fear-response that's ready to trigger at all times, there is no need to layer on more. If you can start to change your beliefs about what makes a winner, that is a start. You could begin to question your beliefs about competing, striving, beating and putting other people down, being better or having more. Are they really useful?

Facing your fear

Once you have a clearer view of your fear, you can calculate the cost it is having in your life.

Is fear changing the tone and quality of the success you experience?

You may feel nothing is ever enough, or satisfying or joyful. You may be engaged in a never-ending pursuit of what's next. You may also fear losing the success you already have. And feel restless and unsatisfied, leaving little room for gratitude or contentment.

What is fear inhibiting you from trying, from starting or from stopping?

Are you a good leader in most ways but reluctant to challenge one respected colleague who you know is a problem? Do you have an unreasonable reluctance to speak openly about yourself? How does fear impact upon your relationships? How does it impact your energy and motivation? And what does it do to your sense of well-being? Has fear stopped you even trying? So you'd rather give up than be exposed as a failure. Or you've thought about resigning from your job rather than face criticism (or actually done this). Or you end a relationship before the other person rejects you.

What is fear doing to your relationships?

This is important; they are probably what matter most in your life. If you don't want other people to know your fears, you may find yourself being guarded or defensive, even bitchy, when anyone gets too close to talking about your fear or makes you feel threatened. Or you might find yourself withdrawing, keeping a level of distance between you and the next person. Or perhaps you are overreactive in your family dynamics or closest relationship because there you feel you can express your emotion (but not why you feel it). Whichever way, you might find it hard to be present — here, in real time, in your relationships.

Facing fear might involve some discomfort as you look inside your own values and sense of identity.

Are you true to who you say you are, or does fear hijack you so you behave, think and feel differently to your core values? If I ask you what you believe in, would your answer fit with how you show up every day for other people? The gap between these two things, who you say you are and how you show up, can be caused by fear.

Replacing your fear

While we can evolve our psychology, fear as part of human nature is impossible to change. It can only be blocked or channelled, and I am suggesting you block it and channel it *deliberately* in favour of enjoying your life more.

The bottom line is that you can steer yourself away from limiting fears and towards something more valuable. There is no magic trick or guaranteed formula, and it's not necessarily quick, but it's real.

It is possible (and in your interests) to rewrite the story you are living. You don't have to write a fairy tale. Just pick up the pen.

To replace fear, start to think in terms of animating your life some more.
Imagine, decide, do, struggle, mess up, renew, look forward, go again.

Say who you are and what you care about, say what you are going for, rather than hedging your bets in case those endeavours go wrong.
Your failures are part of the education you can't get anywhere else. When you look at who you are, you're going to realise there is no comfort zone. Find the thing you can work with and use to fill your spirit. None of us can sell out for security and comfort without risking losing ourselves – we are wild at heart.

Having a strong and enduring purpose in life can also help to direct the way we see things.
It doesn't need to be grand; humble works just as well. You are much more likely to get your game face on each day if you feel purposeful.

It is 100 percent human to imagine, desire and dream.
Dreams are (renewable) rocket fuel for creativity and the psyche. And conformity and logic are overrated when it comes to dealing with fear. One question to ask yourself might be: 'What strengthens your interest in expanding yourself, the world and/or humanity?'

Don't try to wipe the slate clean of your mistakes or mess.

Make your failures and even your pain into a resource. It happened. It hurt. You don't welcome more. But maybe your heartbreak also cracked something else open, revealed some deep emotion and some passion. Passion isn't sensible or neat. It can make you seem unusual or weird, exactly the sort of thing you might prefer to cover up. It can even feel close to madness. But it can also be channelled as a resource to take you beyond fear.

Fear steals your ability to really *be* with other people.

Get connected to – not just associated with – the people in your life. Shift how you open up and relate to them. That means making more room for love in all its forms. We don't have many visible role models for intimacy outside of families, and yet communication, trust and empathy with each other can heal us of fear. Try to be present in your own communities and relationships that nourish your resilience and buffer any *not-good-enough-fear*.

Finally, get back into this moment.

Not-good-enough fears keep you trapped inside your thoughts, lost inside your own head, walking through life like a zombie, never noticing how you feel. Do you taste what you eat? Do you notice you've been holding your breath? Or that your back aches? Regularly coming back to your body and the present moment is grounding and calming, and it cuts any fears down to size. Life is just this moment.

Bibliography

Akala, *Natives: Race and Class in the Ruins of Empire* (Two Roads, 2018)

Hari, J., *Uncovering the Real Causes of Depression – and the Unexpected Solutions* (Bloomsbury, 2018)

Gordon, J., *You Win in the Locker Room* (John Wiley & Sons, 2015)

Marshall, K., *Yellow and Black* (Slattery Media Group, 2018)

Thunberg, G., *No One is too Small to Make a Difference* (Penguin, 2019)

Resources

If you are in urgent need or are thinking of self-harming or suicide, please contact the following agencies:

Samaritans
116 123 (free, 24-hour helpline)
www.samaritans.org.uk

Papyrus (for young people)
HOPELINEUK: 0800 068 4141 (10 a.m. to 10 p.m. Monday to Friday; 2 p.m. to 10 p.m. weekends and bank holidays)
www.papyrus-uk.org

ChildLine
0800 1111
www.childline.org.uk

Other agencies

The NHS website has a comprehensive list of agencies dealing with mental health – see https://www.nhs.uk/conditions/stress-anxiety-depression/mental-health-helplines/ - but here are some ones that deal specificity with stress, anxiety and depression.

Anxiety UK
03444 775 774 (9.30 a.m. to 5.30 p.m. Monday to Friday)
www.anxiety.org.uk

Heads Together
If you need immediate support, text SHOUT to 85258
www.headstogether.org.uk

Mental Health UK
www.mentalhealth-uk.org
England – Rethink Mental Illness
0121 522 7007 (9.30 a.m. to 4.30 p.m. Monday to Friday, excluding bank holidays)
www.rethink.org

Wales – Hafal
01792 816 600 / 832 400 (9 a.m. to 5 p.m. Monday to Friday, excluding bank holidays)
www.hafal.org

Scotland – Support in Mind Scotland
0131 662 4359 (9 a.m. to 5 p.m. Monday to Friday, excluding bank holidays)
www.supportinmindscotland.org.uk

Mental Health Foundation

www.mentalhealth.org.uk

Mind

0300 123 3393 (9 a.m. to 6 p.m., Monday to Friday)

www.mind.org.uk

SANE

SANEline: 0300 304 7000 (4.30 p.m. to 10.30 p.m. daily)

www.sane.org.uk/support

YoungMinds

If you are a young person looking for urgent help, text: 85258
If you are a parent worried about your child, call the Parents
Helpline 0808 802 5544

www.youngminds.org.uk

Notes

Chapter 5: What happens to us in fear culture?

1 Dweck, C., *Mindset* (Robinson, 2012)
2 Akala, *Natives: Race and Class in the Ruins of Empire* (Two Roads, 2018)
3 Brown, B. (2012, 16 March). 'Brené Brown: Listening to shame' [Video file]. Retrieved from http://www.ted.com/talks/brene_brown_listening_to_shame.html

Chapter 6: How (and why) our brains create fear

4 Nadler, R., 'Where did my IQ points go?' viewed September 2019, www.psychologytoday.com/us/blog/leading-emotional-intelligence/201104/where-did-my-iq-points-go

Chapter 7: Bossing in-the-moment fear

5 Unauthored, 2016, 'William Trubridge: New Zealander dives 102m to set freedive world record,' viewed Spetember 2019, www.bbc.co.uk/sport/diving/36856390

6 Unauthored, 'The Shocking Reality of Freediving Death
   Rates,' viewed September 2019, freedivingfreedom.com/
   risks-of-freediving/freediving-death-rates-the-shocking-
   reality/

7 Dancke Skaare, S., 2017, 'Why do we like watching horror
   films,' viewed September 2019, https://partner.sciencenor
   way.no/film-forskningno-inland/why-do-we-like-watching-
   horror-films/1451826

8 Trubridge, W., 'Mental Techniques for 102m,' viewed
   September 2019, http://williamtrubridge.com/writings/
   mental-techniques-for-102m/

9 ibid.

10 ibid.

Chapter 8: Not-good-enough *fear, and how to face it*

11 Chopra, D., 2012, 'The best use of imagination is creativ-
    ity. The worst use of imagination is anxiety' [Twitter],
    viewed September 2019, https://twitter.com/deepakchopra/
    status/250980201360678912?lang=en

Chapter 13: Getting into the mess

12 'Saunders, G., 2014, What We're Loving: Algiers, Aliens,
    Adulthood,' The Paris Review, viewed September 2019,
    www.theparisreview.org/blog/2014/07/25/the-vale-of-soul-
    making/

Chapter 14: Replace fear with a different story

13 Mpanga, G. 2019. *Have You Heard George's Podcast?*
    [Podcast]. [Accessed September 2019]. Available from

https://www.bbc.co.uk/programmes/p07915kd/episodes/downloads

14 Hari, J., *Lost Connections - Uncovering the Real Causes of Depression – and the Unexpected Solutions* (Bloomsbury, 2018)

15 Freeman Yeboah, T. 2018, 'Barack Obama selects ex-Gha naian footballer for Leaders Africa Programme,' Pulse. com, viewed September 2019, https://www.pulse.com.gh/sports/football/barrack-obama-selects-ex-ghanaian-footballer-for-leaders-africa-programme/554r1hm

Chapter 15: Replace fear with purpose

16 Wrack, S., 'Leading Afghan football official banned by Fifa in relation to sexual abuse,' *The Guardian*, viewed September 2019, https://www.theguardian.com/football/2019/oct/11/afghan-football-official-banned-fifa-sexual-abuse-sayed-ali-reza-aghazada

Chapter 16: Replace fear with surrender

17 Bogage, J., 'Messi wore a reporter's good luck charm during Argentina's win,' *The Washington Post*, viewed September 2019, https://www.washingtonpost.com/news/soccer-insider/wp/2018/06/27/did-messis-good-luck-charm-send-argentina-to-the-world-cups-knockout-stage/

Chapter 17: Replace fear with dreams and desires

18 Epstein, M., *Open to Desire* (Avery, 2006)

19 Brooklyn Academy of Music (2015), Jane Goodall on the indomitable human spirit. Available at: https://www.youtube.com/watch?v=ZXQfomDTp3Q

Chapter 18: Replace fear with real connection

20 Hari, J., *Lost Connections – Uncovering the Real Causes of
    Depression and the Unexpected Solutions* (Bloomsbury, 2018)

21 Gordon, J., *You Win in the Locker Room First* (John Wiley &
    Sons, 2015)

22 Marshall, K., *Yellow and Black* (Slattery Media, 2017)

23 ibid.

24 Players' Tribune Global (2017), Trent Cotchin - Defining
    Moment. Available at: https://www.youtube.com/watch?v=
    Dob-KZm1piM

25 Marshall, K., *Yellow and Black* (Slattery Media, 2017)

Acknowledgements

This book is about living a more soulful life by resizing and reshaping our fear. At the very heart of that endeavour is the quality of the relationships we have, with ourselves and with others. I feel like I have had many blessed, extraordinary relationships professionally and personally, and without them no meaningful progress would be made at all. The journey to writing this book, and the many people who lifted and encouraged me, has been testament to that.

I started by feeling like I didn't have the authority to write about such a complex emotion. Then I realised it wasn't authority I lacked; it was the sense of having permission. In the wake of the football World Cup in 2018 there was so much unexpected fanfare and media attention on me – the raised eyebrows about taking too much credit in some corners; the overblown hero-making in others – that I wanted to shrink back and head for cover. I had a screeching desire to keep my head down. I realised over time that holding back was driven by fear and not by desire. When I did find my voice, I saw how useful it was to people who were struggling with feeling not good enough, in all the ways this shows itself. I also realised I cared enough about this to face my own fear and share my ideas with the world.

As always, it took a team. First, the permission and encouragement of my brilliant family and their gentle teasing and love throughout, especially Mum. They are the most real people I know and however tough the journey at times, I'm always glad we did it together. Second, my husband Abdoulaye and my Senegalese family who inspire me regularly and give me another model for fearlessness. Anyone who knows a Senegalese person understands the pride! Third, my endlessly supportive and true friends across continents who I treasure and lean on. For the period of this book I have especially leant on Errol, Jane, Mitch, Shane, Catherine, Isobel, Suzanne and Carrie, and I am tremendously grateful for their love, care and humour.

For his role in being my ally and thinking partner through the World Cup and beyond, I am grateful to Owen Eastwood and, for their generous leadership and open minds, to Gareth Southgate, Brendon Gale, Damien Hardwick, Stephen Kearney and especially Tom Vernon.

For continually opening my mind and reshaping my world view, I owe a great debt to psychologists and professors Dr Mark Anderson, Dr Lori Pye and the Viridis Graduate Institute.

To Rory Scarfe at the Blair Partnership for pushing / dragging me forward and to Joel Rickett and the brilliant team at Ebury for making it seem obvious and inevitable that I should pick up this pen and write: thank you for the partnership and encouragement; I hope this is just the start.

And finally to Brigid Moss, my unfathomably patient editor who has not only stayed on the rollercoaster with me while I freaked out, but kept returning me to what I care about, to keeping it human and grounded and to getting out of my comfort zone more to offer more for the reader. I am more grateful than I can express.